praise for *job hopper*

"Ayun Halliday is the consummate dilettante, dissecting her checkered career with razor wit and a discerning eye for the best absurdities—a bright, beautiful gem of a book." —Mike Daisey, author of *21 Dog Years: A Cube Dweller's Tale*

"Hilarious and painful . . . takes me back to my days of working a series of flunky jobs before I settled on one to keep for thirty-five years." —Harvey Pekar, author of *American Splendor*

"Un(der)paid artiste keeps body and soul together without selling either. And yes, I too scrubbed pit stains out of bunny costumes." —Joyce Brabner, co-author of *Our Cancer Year*

"A truly hilarious lesson in gratitude. Ayun Halliday's misadventures in job land remind us to thank our lucky stars when we finally land a gig that doesn't make us want to hurt ourselves or others. (Not to mention one that doesn't require us to wear panty hose.)" —Ana Gasteyer, actress

also by ayun halliday

No Touch Monkey!
And Other Travel Lessons Learned Too Late

"I laughed hard on nearly every page of this shockingly intimate travel memoir and deeply funny book. Ayun Halliday lives an interesting life, and it's the good luck of us less daring types that she writes it so well."
—Stephen Colbert, *The Daily Show with John Stewart*

"Travelers beware! Written with spunk and fast-flying wit, Ayun Halliday defines the misadventure and shows that getting dirty can be done with grace."
—Jennifer L. Leo, editor of *Sand in My Bra and Other Misadventures*

"[A] self-effacing rant on the humiliations of shoestring travel. . . . Prepare to laugh out loud while commiserating with her new challenges."
—*Toronto Globe & Mail*

"Her collection of travel stories is not just a sweet read, but an abject lesson in what to do when, as they say, 'shit happens.'" —*Austin Chronicle*

The Big Rumpus: A Mother's Tales from the Trenches

"The Great American Tale of one woman's schlep through early motherhood—honest, hilarious, and irresistibly naughty. Ayun Halliday, a highly caffeinated and refreshingly immodest city gal . . . might just become the patron saint of blissfully imperfect motherhood." —Amazon.com

"The lively personality of Halliday's quarterly zine, *The East Village Inky,* comes through in this rambunctious little book that takes a hard-eyed and hilarious look at full-time motherhood in the city. She has a refreshingly irreverent but joyous voice." —*Booklist*

"*The Big Rumpus* is positively the best mothering memoir I've read by a straight-tawkin', breast-feeding, xenophilic, world-traveling, Indiana-reared, New York City transplant. I stayed up past my bedtime reading it, no lie. The gal can write." —*Utne Reader*

"A breezy memoir of motherhood that, for all its hip attitude, also affectingly recalls traditional fears, joys, and a sense of the miraculous."
—*Kirkus Reviews*

job hopper

the checkered career of a down-market dilettante

ayun halliday

Job Hopper: The Checkered Career of a Down-Market Dilettante

"In the Weeds" was originally published as "Dave's Italian Kitchen" in *Women Who Eat: A New Generation on the Glory of Food* (Seal Press, 2003).

AVALON
publishing group incorporated

Published by
Seal Press
An Imprint of Avalon Publishing Group, Incorporated
1400 65th Street, Suite 250
Emeryville, CA 94608

Library of Congress Cataloging-in-Publication Data

Halliday, Ayun.
Job hopper : the checkered career of a down-market dilettante / by Ayun Halliday.
p. cm.
ISBN 1-58005-130-8 (pbk.)
1. Work--Humor. I. Title.

PN6231.W644H36 2004
814'.6--dc22

2004029155

ISBN 1-58005-130-8

9 8 7 6 5 4 3 2 1

Interior and cover design by Amber Pirker
Printed in Canada by Transcontinental
Distributed by Publishers Group West

For the usual suspects

and Dave Glatt

and anyone with the business sense to major in theater.

contents

introduction

© Betsy Harris

It's been at least a decade since I made peace with the fact that I'm too long in the tooth to play Juliet. But only when I started writing this book did it dawn on me that the once-abundant supply of crappy day jobs I could be expected to hold in the future has dwindled to a much more finite figure, something I can count on one hand, or maybe even one thumb. My thirties are drawing to a close, my children are little and far from autonomous, and my playwright husband laid a golden egg a few years back that knocked the wolf a bit farther away from our door.

Call me sentimental, call me perverse, but the reduced probability that I will never draw an hourly wage for having phone sex with credit card–holding strangers seems tragic in a way that my dwindling fertility does not. It's like I suddenly woke up one day and realized that I forgot to get a job at Kinko's. Odds are now I never will. And unless I'm willing to pull a Barbara Ehrenreich, my chances of ringing up patio furniture and bulk toilet paper at Wal-Mart are slim to none. I'd never shop there, but there's an autumnal chill to realizing that I won't work there. I'll never know how things look from the other side of a McDonald's drive-up window. I'll never aim an antifungal aerosol spray at a line of returned bowling shoes. I'll never be able to commiserate, "Yeah, I spent a summer in the Roach Motel factory."

No more free office supplies. No stillborn company picnics. No customer complaints.

"You'll miss this stage when it's over," wistful-eyed older women remark, as my young children and their seemingly endless needs swarm. Why did no one say the same when I was pulling slightly-more-than-minimum wage in the costume warehouse, the lame-ass nightclub, the hippie clothing store, the lowest-common-denominator art gallery, or the dozens of restaurants and offices in which I wreaked mostly unintentional havoc? Unlike the physicians, lawyers, and CEOs who find themselves at loose ends post-retirement, my identity was never defined by what I did for a living. Theater was my life, even if snobbery prevented me from wearing a bright red t-shirt emblazoned with that very claim, a gift from a well-meaning friend of my mother's. So why is it that, writing this book, I started experiencing the day jobber's equivalent of empty nest syndrome?

Experience, age, and the icy cold plunge of procreation have opened my eyes to the fact that we grasshoppers need not spend our entire lives shoehorning ourselves into the anthill. There are plenty of grasshopper jobs, too. Most of them involve emptying spit valves in some way and they rarely cover health insurance, but for those fiddlers content to dwell in domestic bohemia past age forty, they offer a never-to-be-taken-for-granted refuge.

Still, if only I could go back, just for a day, like *Our Town*'s Emily Webb, who having died in childbirth, makes a pit stop at her twelfth birthday before settling into her grave for all eternity.

If only I could surreptitiously photocopy a few hundred flyers for my latest theatrical endeavor, to snag some Liquid Paper, to push my lunch break twenty minutes past its stipulated end time, just for one day. How indescribably sweet. Bittersweet, really. Okay, possibly just bitter.

And like Emily, I might not be able to handle it, especially if I wasn't getting at least eight bucks an hour.

© Martin Drobac

have you ever touched a mastodon bone?

My father used to take me in my stroller to the Children's Museum, back when it was housed in an old mansion in a once-grand neighborhood near downtown Indianapolis. Family lore has him parking me in front of two moth-eaten stuffed polar bears. Apparently, I just couldn't get enough of those things. Every time I saw them, I would get all jacked up, pointing and going, "ooh ooh ooh." I don't remember this, although I do recall the bears from subsequent visits. I also have many pleasant memories of my father pointing and going, "ooh ooh ooh" as he impersonated baby me for all of my boyfriends over the years.

My ursine pals were still on display when I was later hired as a museum security guard, though by that time they had been reassigned to an exhibit that re-created their pre-death surroundings through cunning use of Styrofoam. Before the museum moved into its new multimillion-dollar facility, the bears had been posted at the foot of the mansion's marble staircase, poised as if to devour the ghosts of any upper-class ladies who might come sweeping down in evening dress. Their new location struck me as a social demotion. Educational opportunities abounded in the *Native Americans of the Pacific Northwest* exhibit, but visitors tended to ignore the whole damn wing in favor of sexier, more frenetic attractions, like the top-floor carousel and the hands-on science lab, where children could come to blows over whose turn it was to touch the metal ball that made their hair stand on end. We guards were rotated throughout two dozen or so beats. When I spent the day in the bears' area, it made me sad to see the lukewarm reactions with which they were met. Midwestern families would wander in, gaze about listlessly, and then go right back out, the parents looking hypoglycemic as the kids whined about bathrooms, hot dogs, and each other. Where was my successor, the excitable toddler who would point and go, "ooh ooh ooh"? Wreaking havoc in the gift shop, maybe.

For all its carefully curated dioramas, *Native Americans of the Pacific Northwest* was boring. Even when I was little, in the pre-VCR age, children had no desire to learn about baskets, or even spears. This lack of interest guaranteed a certain funereal hush that was not entirely unwelcome to us guards if, for example, we had spent our prior shift policing the unsupervised screeching shorties barreling down the Guggenheim-like ramps that connected the six floors open to the public. The Pacific Northwest afforded plenty of solitude in which to contemplate every single fact on every single exhibit card, another innovation of the new regime. For a while I amused myself by pretending that I *was* a Native American of the Pacific Northwest, that the whale-oil lamps and wooden seal-bludgeoning clubs behind double thicknesses of Plexiglas belonged to me. When I wearied of that little game, I started sneaking peeks at paperback novels I smuggled in in the pocket of my beige uniform windbreaker, a necessity in the exhibit's subarctic air-conditioning.

That, too, stopped when I was caught completely off guard (as it were) by Orly, the nicer of my two bosses. I harbored a fierce desire to make Orly proud of me, to strike him as something more than a fly-by-night white kid who wouldn't last more than a few months in the uniform. Having caught me red handed, he cleared his throat softly to tear me away from the bullfight I'd been enjoying courtesy of Ernest Hemingway, depositing me back on the industrial-carpeted tundra. I looked up in confusion that was quickly supplanted by shame. Orly tucked his chin into the hollow of his skinny throat to peer at me over the top of his aviator frames, eyebrows lifted in expectation of the gabbling apology he knew was coming. The man had been guarding these birchbark canoes and eyeless beaver pelts since before I was born. I couldn't tell him that two hours into my shift I was so bored that I thought my brain might calcify into a geode if it wasn't allowed a tiny morsel of *The Sun Also Rises.*

Unwilling to risk another bust, I then entered a zone of indescribable tedium. If you've ever spent time in solitary confinement, you'll know what I'm talking about. I checked my watch every sixty seconds, tried to remember the seating arrangement of my second-grade classroom, and practiced standing on one leg with my eyes closed. At a certain angle, the zipper pull on my windbreaker resembled a one-eyed duck's head, a little friend with whom I held conversations. Every job I'd held up until that point—camp counselor, lifeguard, counter girl at Herb's Deli—now struck me, belatedly, as a wonderful premise for a lighthearted teen sex comedy. With the sole exception of my college boyfriend, who was devoting the summer to detassling corn in his hometown in Iowa, my friends still spent their working hours in bathing suits. I could have done that, too, but my head was turned by the museum's hourly wage, a whole buck more than my previous record of $4.75 an hour.

Alone and shivering in the Pacific Northwest, I remembered my lifeguard gig at the pool on the roof of the Vantage House Apartments, and how every morning I'd arrive to find every stick of furniture, including the standing ashtrays, at the bottom of the deep end, courtesy of the partying residents. I silently worked my way through the greatest hits of Gnawbone Camp, from "Today" to "The Titanic." I lovingly recalled setting up the dessert station before Herb's opened for the day, rinsing the gray beards off of moldy strawberries and glazing them with red goo from an industrial-sized can. I counted and recounted how many days were left until school started again. Anything to keep myself from thinking about how the diorama mannequins could come to life and get me. The creepiest tableau was lit by a 20-watt cellophane campfire, realistically stirred by breezes from a hidden fan. I can't tell you how many times I saw the plaster figure squatting near this artificial heat source actually move in the flickering light. It was subtle but sinister, an index finger flexing ever so slightly, the head rotating just the teeniest bit to the left. When Albertine came lumbering in fifteen minutes late to relieve me for my half-hour lunch break, I could have thrown myself against her massive bosom to weep with gratitude.

Punishing tedium was only part of the story. The chinos and beige polo shirt that, together with my beige windbreaker, made up my security guard uniform were wreaking havoc on my self-esteem. It was easier to think of myself as "pleasingly plump" when, like any self-respecting soon-to-be sophomore theater major, I was thundering around in a tattered Edwardian camisole and a floaty hippie skirt. With precious little to distract me from my dumpy beige heiner, unflatteringly reflected in multiple Plexiglas display cases, I resolved to take extreme measures. While the other young guards fed on microwaved nachos from the concession stand and Albertine brought in hampers of home cooking, I made do with a can of chocolate malt–flavored Slim-Fast. I think the only thing more horrible than drinking a prefab diet shake every day for lunch is doing so in a sexless beige uniform in an impersonal, fluorescent-lit break room while the screams of tantrumming children in the Natural Sciences Wing seep through the cinder block walls. The cabinets that lined the break room were all empty, save for a few handfuls of ketchup packets and sporks nicked from the concession stand. The fridge was an odoriferous minefield of unidentified tinfoil wads. The emphasis on stimulation and design that permeated the public areas of the museum was nowhere in evidence in the break room, leading me to wonder if perhaps even Zen monks might not be so Zen without their pretty bowls and attractive shoji screens, if all they had to work with were metal folding chairs, beige plastic surfaces, and an elderly handwritten sign admonishing them to clean up after themselves.

Occasionally, I would find myself "eating" lunch at the same time as Winnie or Deana, who thought I was nice even if I was "arty," or Charlesetta and DeShawn, who liked it that I wasn't stuck-up even though I was white. Those were heady times. However, much more frequently I'd find myself sharing the break room with Orly's mean counterpart, Bryce, and maybe one of the old ladies from the gift shop. The existential despair this Sartrean combination inspired only increased when I drew the straw for early lunch, leaving me at break's close with another six hours to go until quitting time. If I'd been really smart, I'd have figured out that there's a way to make quitting time come much faster: namely, to quit. I'll bet with a little legwork I could have found some condo complex still in search of a lifeguard. Instead, I toughed it out with a chalky liquid lunch that produced no discernible weight loss. Eventually, I relocated from the break room to a small patch of lawn far from the visitors' entrance. Some low shrubs formed a convenient hideout, a little enclosure that prevented passing motorists—like, say, anyone I had gone to high school with—from glimpsing me in all my beige, Slim-Fasting glory. If I racewalked up and down the ramps to and from my post, I could log twenty-six minutes of coveted alfresco reading time. It was like a return to identity.

"You got ice cream in that can?" A disembodied head peeked over the top of the manicured hedge. Oh hell, a kid.

"No," I said, smiling lamely. "I wish."

"Then what it be?" he asked, entering my private nook on his hands and knees.

"Oh, it's just something for grownups. It's *supposed* to be like a milkshake, but it's not. Trust me." Deciding that the disparity in our ages relieved me of compulsory small talk, I rested my head on my poly-blend knees. I wondered what it was like to detassle corn. Seemed like it could be kind of fun, riding out to the shed before sunrise in the back of an old pickup, maybe saving a couple of husks to make dolls. Too bad Ray and I couldn't have spent the summer on campus. We could've gotten jobs together, maybe in a restaurant. I was an *actress,* after all! I should be waitressing! And Ray was a Russian major. What business had he out in the cornfields? We could be together, sneaking french fries off of our customers' plates before carrying them out of the kitchen, just like Bill Murray and Dustin Hoffman in *Tootsie!*

"Ain't no milkshake?" the kid asked, blowing a big hole in the dyke meant to keep grim reality from invading my reverie.

"Nope."

"Dag." Scowling on my behalf, he shook his head and flipped the latch on a battered Batman lunch box. Inside, several fistfuls of Cheerios rattled around loose. He shoved some in his mouth and grinned. "You like Cheerios?"

"No, too plain. I used to like Count Chocula."

"I like Cheerios. They good." He ate some more, unconcerned.

"Does your mommy know you're out here?" He looked at me blankly. "Your daddy? Or your babysitter? Your grandma?" He squinted at the cloudless sky, scratching the peeling *Star Wars* decal on his T-shirt as he considered. I envied him his freedom of dress. My break was sifting away from me like hourglass sand. "Who did you come here with today?" I demanded, exasperated.

He erupted in gap-toothed mirth. "Myself!" he crowed.

I wondered if I should take him to the information desk—could I be penalized for tardiness when I relieved my relief person? "So, you just came by yourself?" He nodded, rooting through his Cheerios with an index finger until he found one to his liking. He placed it on his tongue carefully, like a communion wafer or a tab of acid. "Uh, how old are you?"

"Eight. My name is Rolls Royce Jackson. I live at Sixteen Oh Two North Capitol," he recited in a high-pitched staccato.

"That's right around here, isn't it?" I asked. Rolls Royce shot me a withering look and pointed across the parking lot. "Okay, well, I've got to go back to work. You're okay here by yourself?"

"Can I have your can?"

"It's empty. I drank it all. I swear, it isn't what you think it is."

"I know. I just like the picture."

Roycie wasn't the only unsupervised child to treat the museum as an air-conditioned summer camp. Each of the younger guards had a devotee among the neighborhood children, an adoring pet to be plied with candy and quarters. When Winnie worked the information desk, she allowed Carpenter, who at four was the baby of the gang, to nestle in her lap. There were a couple of preteen sisters who apparently lived to make up dance routines, which they then performed for Charlesetta, and the community college–bound DeShawn had made it his mission to set a fatherly example for Roycie. My special friend was a dainty eight-year-old named Angela, who overlooked the overwhelming beigeness of my appearance to pay lavish tribute to my shoes, my earrings, and the John Lennon–style glasses I had to wear after my contact lens scratched my cornea. She lived in hope that she might be permitted to braid my hair, an eventuality I kept postponing. Although Orly allowed our little friends to hang around and hold hands with their favorite guards, I suspected he would draw the line at beauty parlor.

The vast majority of the pale-skinned thousands who poured through the entrance every week qualified as uptighty whities, with one notable exception: the Mennonites who drove down from Shipshewana. Mothers who admonished their children for staring at wheelchair-bound visitors gaped openly at the white bonnets on the women and the strange dustmop-shaped beards on the men. The Mennonites were having way too much fucking fun to rankle under such impolite scrutiny. They exuded high-box social spirits as they swarmed through the Reuben Wells, an out-of-commission steam engine that hulked in the basement. The men discussed the workmanship on the planes and awls scattered around the Indiana pioneers' covered wagon, while the women hit the log cabin to check out the quilts. Everybody from Grandma to Baby Hiram took a mirthful spin on the Please Touch butter churn. It warmed the cockles of my disillusioned heart. I had seen a lot of Parkay-faced unpleasantness on the re-created prairie, most of it revolved around the butter churn. I was enduring crushing boredom and a synthetic sackcloth uniform in order for children to have a fun-filled educational experience, not so that every crew-cut boy with a sports-themed tank shirt and sugar-heavy diet could masturbate that poor churn into a lather, whooping like the rednecks that rape Ned Beatty in *Deliverance.* I'd have suspended my distaste for corporeal punishment—nay, I'd have paid good money to see a Mennonite take the willow switch to one of those brats, but whenever the troublemakers' parents whacked them upside their heads for some unrelated offense, I nursed unhealthy revenge fantasies that seethed alarmingly close to the surface. I imagined myself attacking those whey-faced mommies and daddies with the butt end of my walkie-talkie, kicking ass while Tiffany and Tyler wailed from the rustic porch. "This museum was put here for your enjoyment!" I'd roar as I wrestled them to the industrial carpeting. "Show some respect!" Naturally, in this version of Armageddon, the Mennonites were spared. My tireless vigilante efforts would clear the way for a New Museum Order in which Mennonites and neighborhood children were given free reign to handle the items formerly displayed behind Plexiglas and guards in purple gauze would occasionally glance up from their books to smile benevolently.

Would that it were true. Christ almighty, did every yahoo who posed for a picture with the churn have to pull some goofy face or, just as bad, refuse to smile so that everyone would know what a sucky time they had had with their families at the Children's Museum? The Mennonites didn't have cameras, though I was pretty sure they had butter churns. Apparently, familiarity didn't breed contempt with them. Nothing seemed to—not even the mastodon bone stationed on an otherwise display-free stretch between galleries. Typifying the easy yet empty rewards of our fast-food culture, the plywood board to which the bone was mounted presented passersby with this challenge: HAVE YOU EVER TOUCHED A MASTODON BONE? Not HAVE YOU EVER TOUCHED A MASTODON BONE AND THEN STUCK AROUND TO READ ALL THE SMALL PRINT SO YOU'LL KNOW WHAT THE HELL A MASTODON WAS AND FROM WHAT PART OF ITS BODY THIS BONE WAS HARVESTED? A hundred years ago, hand-to-mastodon-bone contact would have occasioned a flurry of commentary on postcards and in diaries. Now, it's just something to spank and forget about en route to the snack bar—unless you're Mennonite, of course. Maybe the administration had been squeezing the curators for more PLEASE TOUCH displays to satisfy some grant's quota. What else would move someone to bolt that lonely bone to that dumb board when its logical resting place was in the DinoZone, at the feet of the life-size *T. rex,* who from certain angles bore an uncanny resemblance to Jimmy Durante? Actually, fuck the DinoZone. In the infinitely preferable, post-apocalyptic Children's Museum in my mind, any neighborhood child or Mennonite who spent more than fifteen minutes drawing a picture of a dinosaur would be given a complimentary mastodon bone to take home as a little prize to spur on the spirit of scientific inquiry.

It wasn't like we couldn't afford to give some away to deserving members of the public. There were hundreds more bones warehoused in Collections, a cavernous space which was off-limits to the peons of the museum staff, guards included. I got a peek once when I was yanked off active duty to type up some information cards for Seymour, the restorations expert. You had to walk through Collections to get to Seymour's lair, which he kept well stocked with coffee, cassette tapes, and hundreds of teeny-tiny paintbrushes, some of which contained just a single bristle. He put me in mind of Gepetto with his leather apron and his shock of white hair. I liked to think of him doing routine maintenance on Pinocchio as he whistled along to "Let It Bleed." Seymour could repair anything: an ancient pair of beaded moccasins, a shattered teapot, a vintage Wurlitzer jukebox on whose glass face some historically minded young visitor, evading the elephantine Albertine's gaze, had managed to scrawl "Tracy Sucks David R's Dick." The whole time I was typing up those cards, I fantasized about how great it would be to be Seymour's assistant, to bid goodbye to beige and to the tedium of standing in one place for hours, dreaming about clobbering people with my walkie-talkie. Unfortunately, Seymour wasn't in the market for an apprentice, though he did reward my enthusiasm by letting me play in Collections for the rest of the day, notifying Orly and Bryce that he had underestimated the amount of time needed to type up his notes.

On the pleasure meter, browsing Collections rivaled thrift shopping. I wandered around the industrial metal shelving units, picking up items to examine at random. With no brightly colored educational signs to parse out information and no hierarchy of display, the thrill of the hunt was keen. I wondered about every object, who had owned it and how it had wound up on these battleship-gray shelves. Due to the tax-deductible nature of charitable donations, once they came in, they never went out, except as loaners to other museums. It was a bit sad to see the rows full of enough tops, teddy bears, and model boats to brighten at least a hundred orphanages' worth of underprivileged children. Angela would have been over the moon to get her mitts on the china baby dolls that lay sheathed in lacy Victorian christening gowns. What if every neighborhood child was allowed ten minutes in Collections to select just one item to keep? Bet none of them would have picked no sorry-ass old bone.

I found the repetitive rigors of the job even harder to swallow after my half-day hiatus in Collections. Everything about the carefully constructed displays displeased me; plus, Orly and Bryce kept sticking me in The Pursuit of Happiness. Devoted to America's pastimes throughout history, this brightly lit gallery was an aspirin executive's wet dream. It gave one the feeling of being inside a pinball machine, partly because a soundtrack of bleeps, blips, and wildly flapping flippers issued at top volume from speakers hidden in a nonfunctional pinball machine stationed near the entrance. Competing with the pinball machine were an endless loop tape of the Andrews Sisters singing "Boogie Woogie Bugle Boy," an endless loop excerpt of Gomer Pyle, a player piano, the clacking of a toy roller coaster that shot overhead *sans cesse,* and a sprightly Gay Nineties tune accompanying a slide show of Hoosiers indulging in non-drug-related recreational activities. A wooden swing beckoned from a porch that had been installed along one wall, because what could be more relaxing, more typically American, than creaking back and forth, listening to your kids lobbing football helmets and other PLEASE TRY ON sporting equipment at the fun house mirrors erected in the industrial carpeted "yard"?

The only good thing to come out of The Pursuit of Happiness was a yellow Post-it note that a very young child had dictated to his mother and affixed to the Joke Wall. Most of the funnies that found their way onto the wall were the old groaners that used to be printed on the side of Dixie cups, plus a few raunchy, soon-to-be-removed butt-centric contributions from the butter-churn boys. The whole thing was problematic. The Post-its the museum supplied didn't stick properly, and the pencils openly invited vandals. But one day, when I was staring haggardly at the joke wall, wondering when the hell Albertine would arrive to offer me a brief respite from this chaos, I chanced upon this riddle:

> Q: WHAT HAS EIGHT LEGS AND
> CRAWLS?
> A: A SPIDER.

To this day it's the best joke I've ever heard, with the possible exception of the one that ends with the fourth nun asking the third nun, "Excuse me, Sister, do you mind if I gargle before you stick your butt in there?" I love the simplicity of it, the adherence to form coupled with a total lack of comprehension. A spider! How Zen!

"Can we do something about them jokes in Happiness?" one of the older guards carped at morning meeting. "The things some of them kids write would get them a smack on the fanny in my house, I can tell you that!" Everyone sighed. These daily assemblies were torturous enough without Doris Jean launching into one of her lengthy, faith-based complaints. I didn't understand why we couldn't have a dry-erase board in the break room instead of these obligatory pre-business-hours gatherings in which Orly doled out our posts du jour and Bryce belittled us for a never-ending series of minor infractions. If Doris Jean, with her permanently downturned mouth, disproportionately wide bottom, and tight home permanent, was a recognizable Midwestern type, Bryce was another, the mean-spirited middle manager in short polyester dress sleeves. I'd never made the connection before coming to work at the museum, but these two types often sport identical hairstyles, regardless of gender. Perhaps that was why Doris Jean was the only person in security who could tolerate him. She even flirted with him. The rest of us, especially DeShawn and his bespectacled sidekick, Edwin, couldn't stand him. Their mothers had raised them to be suspicious of guys like Bryce in positions of authority.

"You hear how he talk to Royce and them?" Edwin would say, putting down his baloney on white as he affected Bryce's unfriendly smile. "'You run along home now, bwah. Don't know what you think we're trahn t'do here. This int yur personal jungle gym.'" DeShawn, who could not do Caucasian voices, bent over double at the accuracy of the imitation.

I laughed, too, giddy that fortune, as personified by Orly, had arranged for me to find such fine company in the break room on a day too rainy to dine alfresco. "Yeah, Bryce is an asshole," I agreed, unsacking my can. "He should realize that part of the museum's mission is to serve the community."

DeShawn and Edwin chuckled. "Listen to her! 'The community'!"

Oh my god, had I offended them? The museum really did list serving the community as part of the mission statement they included in the donation solicitations that my mother, as a board member, received. But what if my casual use of the term had marked me in my coworkers' eyes as a lip-service liberal, full of shinola, just slumming for the summer before returning to my fancy-pants college, where I would study not nursing or computers, but theater? Theater! DeShawn and Edwin didn't have the luxury of becoming actresses or waitresses! What if they ended up in the museum for good, like Orly and Albertine, prisoners of the beige uniform and the sinister dioramas? To the best of my knowledge, Winnie was the only one of the young guards slated to stay on past August, but what had I done? I scrabbled to rephrase.

"Damn, maybe you wouldn't be so jumpy if you ate some real food," Edwin observed, squinting dubiously at my daily ration of Slim-Fast as he reoriented his Fritos bag so that the opening lay near my hand.

"'Serve the community,'" DeShawn savored. "Actually, though, me and Winnie were talking; maybe before the summer's over, some of us guards could get together after work and take the kids out for ice cream or something like that."

"Off the clock?" Edwin yelped. "You crazy? I got places to go, people to see."

"I'm serious. Do something fun. Ball game or something." I nodded enthusiastically, perhaps less excited by the possibility of doing something special for Angela than significantly grateful to be let off what I feared was a hook. "What'd you do for fun when you were little, Ayun?"

"Hmm," I mused. "Well, I used to line up a bunch of acorns and grass on the stoop that led up to our house and pretend I was a bank teller." My co workers howled. "I went to camp, too!"

"No, I mean, where'd your parents take you," DeShawn said patiently.

"Oh! Uh, they took me here, to the Children's Museum. I'm told I used to point at the polar bears and go, 'ooh, ooh, ooh.'" I looked at them, they looked at me, and then all three of us collapsed in the hilarity of the temporarily condemned, who know that in forty-five seconds they'll have to trudge back up the ramp to their appointed posts—but that in just two weeks they'll be free.

"Dag, who say white people don't know how to have fun," Edwin grimaced, exchanging a triumphant high-five with DeShawn.

yesterday's soup

"You seem like you catch on real quick," Kyle, the head-waiter, drawled as he led me around the dining room, going over the menu and teaching me how to operate the coffeemaker. "That's good, because," he shot a glance at the dun-colored saloon doors leading to the kitchen and lowered his voice, "between you and me, I won't be around much longer. I told Gene when he hired me, I'm not going to stay here forever. We used to be lovers, you know." Using a teaspoon as a hand mirror, he readjusted the complex swirl of his forelock. "He's got to understand that it's time for me to follow my own rainbow, you know? I've already got four colored women working for me part-time."

My eyes widened.

"Oh, I'm sorry, we're not supposed to call them that any-more, are we?"

"Uh," I stalled heroically.

"I hope I didn't offend you," Kyle said, nibbling on a lemon slice he'd customized with half a packet of Equal. "I'm just a country boy."

"I'm from Indiana," I volunteered, by which I meant that I'd be delighted, nay, wildly relieved, to talk cows and corn—not that I was giving his casual racism my Hoosier blessing.

"Indiana? I always forget which one that is." His eyes closed under the weight of geographical recall. "Is it near Michigan?"

"It's right next to Illinois. You can drive there from here in less than forty-five minutes."

"Oh, is it a part of the Indiana Dunes?"

"The Indiana Dunes are in Indiana, yes."

"Oh, me!" Pursing his lips, he stood arms akimbo in a parody of an exasperated mother, perhaps his own. "You must think I'm just a simple country boy!"

My smile was noncommittal. Finished with setup, we now stood shoulder to shoulder, facing the door, awaiting our first customers. Men streamed past the window; six o'clock on a Friday night, and Boys Town was hopping. "Mmm, check that out across the street," Kyle purred, polishing his upper teeth with his tongue in a manner I found most disturbing in a manager. A fit young man in purple terry-cloth short-shorts was bending over to unlock his bike. "I love tight buns," Kyle whispered. Hell, what simple country boy doesn't? I think I detected a bump in aftershave fumes as he slipped his hand inside his dress shirt to caress a nipple.

"So, are you starting your own restaurant, then?" Kyle met my inquiry with the blank look of someone interrupted in the act of masturbation. "You said that you might be leaving? That you have, uh, four women working for you?"

"Oh, mercy." Rolling his eyes, Kyle laughed and rapped

his knuckles against his temple to remind me of his rural simplicity. "No, I've got a little housekeeping business that I'm going full-time with. I'm having a hard time deciding on the name, though."

"What are the contenders?"

"Well, it already has a name: Twinkle Plenty. But I'm thinking of changing it to something more upscale."

"Such as . . . ?"

"Sparkle Much."

The food at Turman's was great, but the service was kind of crappy. For example, I once responded to a concerned regular's inquiry about my recent absence with a blow-by-blow description of my bladder infection. I was just so flattered that he'd noticed I'd been out sick. A fastidiously groomed West Highland white terrier of a man, he dined alone every Wednesday and returned on Fridays with two or three friends, his treat. He made a point of always requesting me as his server. We waiters were sort of like The Beatles, in that each of us had a distinct and loyal following. Hard-bodied, swishy young players from the nearby bars were Kyle men; older, more reserved customers appreciated my college-educated, biologically female femininity; Bernie was Ringo; and Horse snapped up all the leather daddies tanking up on French Provincial comfort food before a big night out at the Manhole. With the exception of the militant vegetarian whose love of Turman's menu seemed only to strengthen his conviction that we'd spike the food with MSG the minute his attention flagged, I felt very attached to my regulars. It was thrilling when these fond feelings seemed reciprocal. I was so moved that Friday when Mr. West Highland White asked after my health, it seemed only fitting to reward him with complete disclosure. By the weak light of no. 3's votive candle, the blood drained from his close-shaven cheeks. I'd never intended for the specter of my burning lady parts to blow a gaping, infected hole in his quiet evening of veal medallions and rarefied observations concerning Wedgwood, corgis, and the vocal stylings of Miss Peggy Lee. I will tell you that the old saw about learning from our mistakes applied here: Even though I worked at dozens of restaurants after Turman's, I never once bothered a customer or client with the grisly details of any infection below the waist.

The indecencies of Turman's service didn't rest entirely on my shoulders. Kyle could perform his duties with a somnambulist's grace, but all pretense of refinement hit the bricks the moment he opened his mouth.

> Customer Contemplating Dessert: "Can you tell me a little more about this 'triple-layer Ghirardelli gateau with mocha-fudge ganache'?"
> Kyle, *after much consideration*: "*Wellll* . . . it's a brown cake with brown icing."

Who wouldn't go for that at seven dollars a slice?

The wait staff was further hobbled by the self-defeating stinginess of Gene Turman, the depressive, shy owner who had given the restaurant his name. Other restaurant owners I'd worked for showboated around in pinkie rings, comping friends and family, rarely picking up so much as a whisk in the kitchen. They bragged and strutted and fired me for not wearing a slip when I hostessed a sunny brunch shift. Gene toiled silently alongside the rest of the kitchen staff, his gloom putting a damper on the backstage banter. Word was he had opened Turman's in retaliation against the former lover with whom he had owned a windowless bistro ten blocks to the north. The bistro was still open for business, serving the very menu Gene had boosted for Turman's—everything from the brown cake with brown icing to the Cornish pasty, justly celebrated in both locations.

"Do you think I could get the recipe for these muffins?" I asked Pixie, the enormous bald cook, as I leaned against the counter, feeding from a Tupperware container of day-olds recovered from the previous night's bread baskets.

"Oh sweetie, there ain't nothing to those but yesterday's soup!" he screamed, his muscles bulging like Popeye's as he hoisted a ten-gallon stockpot onto a back burner. "Miss Eugenia's so tight she's got us stretching her muffin batter with leftover chowder! Tacky. Does make 'em nice and moist, though. I just keep waiting for him to tell me to start dumping the leftover muffins in yesterday's soup! Ha! *Comprende,* Ernesto?"

Realizing that he'd been called upon to support some American opinion, the Ecuadorean dishwasher turned from the sink and nodded mildly. Pixie pulled on the corners of his raffish handlebar mustache until it achieved the defeated droopiness of the one belonging to his friend and boss. Ernesto grinned. "Ees Gene."

"*Sí,* ees Gene," Pixie said approvingly. "Now watch, Ernesto. Gene—" he pulled his mustache tips down again, "Tell Pixie—" he tapped his chest pleasantly, then lunged for a butcher knife, "YOU PUT MUFFIN IN THE SOUP!" Ernesto froze, anxiety roiling behind the obliging smile he assumed whenever one of the gringos tried to interact with him on non-dish-related matters. Realizing that he'd pushed it too far, Pixie immediately dropped the knife and flipped his scarred palms up in an attitude of surrender. "Just kidding, Ernesto. Mr. Gene no make Pixie put muffins in soup. *No problema,* okay?"

"Okay, *no problema,*" Ernesto smiled, returning his attention to the sink. With very few words of English to counterbalance his coworker's near-total lack of Spanish, Ernesto's good disposition went unquestioned. The lone heterosexual on staff until yours truly came along, he spent his one morning off a week at Mass. I don't know what he was praying for, but I don't think it was for the Lord to grant him the strength to come out of the closet, not when he had six children back in his village in Ecuador. What did he make of all those rainbow flags flapping in Boys Town? Pixie's opinion was that most of the oh-Mary high jinks went over Ernesto's head, possibly because the waiters took care to shield him from their smuttier banter, as if he were a c-h-i-l-d who might pick up on their i-n-t-o-n-a-t-i-o-n-s even if he couldn't speak E-n-g-l-i-s-h. Ernesto gained extra points for never taking part in the intramural bitch fights that flared whenever a staff member felt overburdened, unappreciated, or unfairly seated. He was always cheerful, except when there was some disaster—an entire six-top sending back their pork loins, say—in which case he appeared suitably grave. Gene, who was so cheap he once refused to let a pediatric cardiologist place a local call from the restaurant's phone after she'd been beeped with an emergency midway through her mahi-mahi, was rumored to be putting more than one of the six children through school. No matter how crappy a night I might be having, it always gave me a lift when Ernesto ventured out to the waiter's station to refill his coffee mug, a former employee's castoff bearing the motto So Many Men . . . So Little Time!

Of all the many establishments in Boys Town, Turman's kept the lowest, and most frumpy, profile. It was one of those places that people walk by for years without ever registering its existence. Each of the waiters had suggestions for interior redesigns, everything from framed Tom of Finland prints to replacing the faux-burlap wallpaper with thousands of dollars' worth of pink watered silk, but Gene was stubborn in his tastes. He liked the homely macramé-and-driftwood "sculptures" on the burlap walls. He also insisted that we keep the stereo tuned to lite FM, especially after a reggae tape I brought from home sent an elderly early bird fumbling for his nitroglycerin with the lyric, "Suck on your vagina, uh, uh."

Lunch was even deader than we expected the day of the Pride Parade. Pixie sent Ernesto home and told me he'd cook me anything I wanted from the menu. "Surprise me," I said, wanting everything. Most of what we served, I'd never tasted, not officially, since Gene wouldn't let us have anything but salad, soup, or quiche with one ingredient. If it hadn't been for the occasional surreptitious nibble from the tidy remains of Mr. West Highland White's plate, I might well have been reduced to describing those succulent veal medallions as "brown circles in brown sauce." What was Pixie fixing? The insides of my mouth grew noticeably moister as I contemplated the possibilities. Three minutes later, he returned, bearing a platter on which gleamed fifteen strips of bacon.

"Don't look at me like that, child," he chuffed, untying his apron as he joined me at a window table. "You think Auntie doesn't see the way you look at that pig meat every time she's prepping for spinach salad? Just pray Miss Eugenia doesn't come in here and catch you." He put his feet up on a chair and lit a cigarette, jerking his chin toward a gaggle of heavyset men in Dolly Parton wigs and Brazilian bikinis. "Sun must have fried those tacky-ass queens' brains."

"Thish great, Pixie," I said, cramming one piece in hard on the heels of another. I wasn't very worried about getting caught; something told me that Gene most likely spent the Pride Parade holed up in his apartment muttering like Eeyore. "Fanks."

With a dismissive wave, Pixie ashed into his coffee cup.

Customers who asked for ashtrays were informed that the proprietor of the establishment enforced a strict no-smoking policy, an edict that went no farther than the saloon doors leading to the kitchen. "You don't have to thank me. Just eat up all your bacon, baby, or you ain't getting no fudge sauce." Wow, he *had* been keeping an eye on me.

We lolled in the window all afternoon, watching the spectacle roll up Halsted. "Look, there's Horse," I cried, waving frantically as my fellow waiter rode past astride the Manhole's float, wearing nothing but a pair of cowhide chaps.

"Someone ought to slap some sense into that bitch's head," Pixie chuckled fondly.

An elderly Asian woman rounded the corner and froze, holding tight to her paper grocery bag as the spangled, G-stringed crowd swarmed around her. "It's the Occidental nightmare," I said.

Pixie barked in appreciation. "That's what I like about you, child. You're not one of these empty-headed bar fags Miss Eugenia persists in hiring. You, Ernesto, and I are the only ones who know our ass from our elbow."

I brushed the compliment off modestly. "I'm just a simple country boy." No need to tell him I wasn't entirely sure what "Occidental" meant. Apparently, it applied.

A short time later, Kyle finally made good on his threat to devote himself fully to Twinkle Much. Knowing that Bernie/Ringo would be leaving soon to attend nursing school, I assumed that the job of headwaiter was mine. Horse had been there longer, but given that it routinely took him five minutes to total up a check, we both agreed there was no way he'd be promoted. Every time I banged through the double doors to pick up an order, I expected Gene to say something to make it official. The closest he came was, "You're cutting the bread pudding too thick."

When Gene filled the headwaiter's spot with his old friend Miss Thing instead of me, Pixie's displeasure translated into a lot of banging. Ernesto and I cringed as a big metal spoon sailed across the prep table into an empty stainless steel bowl. "Child, I am just about at the end of my tether," the cook spat, as he Lizzie Bordened a cluster of root vegetables with the meat cleaver. "I told Miss Eugenia if she wants to run her restaurant into the ground with her pigheadedness, that's her business, but if he expects me to stand idly by while he brings that fossilized old queen in to—"

"Maybe he wanted someone with managerial experience," I mumbled, reaching into the refrigerator for the tub of muffins.

"Managerial experience, my Aunt Fanny!" Pixie snorted. "The only experience that bloodsucker's got is leeching off his boyfriend. You know the Gilt Canary?" I shook my head. "Oh please, it's that tack-tack-tacky antique store on Broadway, the one with that yappy little Pekingese in the window. Miss Thing's boyfriend owns it, only ceramic greyhounds must be on the way out if Miss Thing's coming around here, hitting Gene up for a regular paycheck." I'd never heard Pixie refer to the boss as Gene before.

"It's okay, Pixie," I said softly. Miss Thing was right on the other side of the saloon doors, examining his manicure in the back booth. I wondered if I was supposed to show him how to work the coffeemaker, the way Kyle had shown me.

"Don't you dare say it's okay," Pixie threatened, leveling the cleaver at me. "I'm sick of the way every faggot who Miss Eugenia used to sleep with or would like to sleep with or should never have slept with in the first place can waltz right in here and get hired regardless of experience or ability. Don't look at me like that! The only exceptions are you and Ernesto." Ernesto glanced up from a mound of potatoes. "It's okay, Ernesto, I was just saying to Ayun that Gene's a crazy old fairy who's trying to drive me crazy, too. *Muy loco, comprende?*"

Ernesto laughed appreciatively. "You good *español,*" he said, giving Pixie a big thumbs-up.

"I'm glad someone's got their head screwed on straight," Pixie muttered darkly, returning to the stove.

Dumb as he was, Kyle had been one of us, grunting through his fair share of sidework and problem tables. I hadn't begrudged the simple country boy the extra dough he got, having suspected even before Pixie confirmed it that he was being rewarded for being an intimate of Gene's as much as for putting receipts into a manila envelope at the end of the night and hanging onto the extra key. Not only did he make me feel smart in comparison, but he always gave me the Sunday paper he bought solely for the TV section.

Unlike his predecessor, Miss Thing wasted no opportunity to take his title at face value, exempting himself from anything he deemed "busboy work," which might not have created such resentment if Turman's *had* busboys. He snapped his fingers when water glasses ran low, stonewalled when the carpet needed sweeping, and told me to get a rag when one of his customers complained that some dust from the driftwood wall sculptures had sifted down into his pumpkin bisque. After a couple of weeks of this, Horse and I decided to present a united front, showing up fifteen minutes early by prearrangement to complain to the real boss about how the rules had changed. Gene didn't even look up from the swordfish he was dismembering, just asked us if we really thought he could be expected to handle every little problem that arose. "He's depressed," Horse whispered as we trudged back through the saloon doors.

"So, what, we're supposed to bus Miss Thing's tables until someone slips him a Valium?" I demanded, as I copied the specials onto the back of my pad. "I'm going to put in an application at Leona's or Ann Sather's or something. You should, too."

"No, I have plans. *Gay Chicago* is writing a story about this friend of mine who makes restraint beds, and he says that as soon as it's published, he'll have more work than he can handle, and he'll be able to take me on as his apprentice."

In the meantime, it fell to us to take any table Miss Thing deemed too ugly, too bitchy, or too cheap to be worthy of his lackluster service. "Woof, woof," he whispered in my ear as he handed off a heavy-bottomed table for one.

I lay awake at night, hatching a scheme whereby I'd corner him in the Gilt Canary and threaten him at close range with the jagged neck of a ceramic greyhound whose head I'd dramatically smashed against the wall only moments before.

Common restaurant wisdom holds that when quitting time grows nigh, the waiter whose tables empty first is the one who gets to fly the coop, leaving the others to wait to see if they'll be cursed with last-minute walk-ins. For instance, the couple who entered late one night, pushing a stroller and laughing happily about having made it in before ten o'clock, should have gone to Miss Thing, who still had entrées working. Not, by any means, to me, who had unpinned my hair and shucked my apron the second my last customer's chair scraped back.

"They're yours," Miss Thing decreed.

"What?" I gestured at the orange plaid minidress that had replaced my waiter's drab. "All I have left to do is hand in my totals. You've still got three tables; plus, I can guarantee that the one in the window is going to want coffee and dessert."

"Psychic, are we?"

"No, but I've probably waited on him a hundred times." I'd have been waiting on him still if I'd had the sense to keep my urinary business private.

Miss Thing poured himself a cup of coffee. "Suit up. I don't do babies."

Ah, but he did do cocaine and criminally minded youth. To make a long story short, Pixie called bright and early the next day to say he'd never ask me to come in on my day off if it weren't an emergency, and that he'd fill me in when I got there. Apparently, after Miss Thing locked up, he'd gone for a few drinkies at Roscoe's around the corner, where he made the acquaintance of a foxy young thing who accompanied him back to Turman's. There they indulged in a couple of kinds of blow until Miss Thing passed out on the kitchen counter, which is where Pixie found him when he arrived to make the muffins. The cash box was empty. "That little hustler made off with over a thousand dollars," Pixie hissed, shrugging his brawny shoulders in distaste. "*Más* Clorox, Ernesto. I don't even want to *think* about what happened on this poor countertop."

"That's terrible. Poor Gene," I said, helping myself to a handful of smoked turkey, then some blueberries, then a spoonful of hard sauce, imagining what a judicious manager I would make. "Is he going to sue Miss Thing or just fire him?"

Pixie groped for his smokes among the spice bottles above the stove. "Child, you're way too smart for your own good, but you've got a lot to learn. Want Mama to fry you up some bacon?"

can you tell me how to get to sesame street?

The department-store woman left us alone to get dressed in a storeroom. "Don't dawdle, though. Doors open at nine and some of those people have been waiting since seven." Nate and I knelt to unzip the footlocker-sized bags that we'd found in the trunk of the van his agency had rented for us for the long drive to the suburban mall. I wished that we'd stopped for coffee on the way. "Holy shit," Nate whispered as we contemplated the impressive, eerie contents. "Which one do you want to be?"

"I have no preference."

"I'll be Ernie. You be Bert. Are you going to leave your underwear on?"

"Yes, aren't you?"

"I don't know. If Janet had told me we were going to be wearing tights, I'd have brought a jockstrap."

"The tights are just so your own skin doesn't show," I said, sitting down on a box to stretch a mustard-colored pair over my bare feet. "You'll have his pants on over them." I suited up in a long-sleeved leotard the same color as the tights, green trousers, and a perfect copy of Bert's vertical-striped jersey. For shoes, I had two toaster-sized soft-sculpture high-tops that swaddled my feet like miniature sleeping bags. "Look, Nate, four fingers," I said, showing him my fuzzy, mustard-colored glove-hands.

"Put your head on." The moment I did, Nate whooped in delighted recognition. "Oh my god, that's insane! Can you see okay?"

"Not too good."

"What?" His voice sounded very far away.

"The mesh is like six inches from my eyes."

"What?"

"God, I hope this isn't going to activate my claustrophobia. What if I freak out?"

"I can't understand a fucking thing you're saying."

"Man, it's really stuffy under there," I gasped, shucking the head.

"Seventy-five bucks an hour for two hours," Nate reminded me before plopping Ernie's head over his own, as determined as a Titanic-era deep-sea diver.

The limited visibility became disorienting almost to the point of motion sickness as the department-store woman, Nate, and I slowly threaded our way through the children's department, holding hands. Racks of play clothes rocked crazily in and out of frame as I tried to sneak a peek at the multitudes. I was experiencing a strange hybrid of stage fright and that hopeless God-I-wish-I-was-finished-instead-of-starting feeling I used to get when clocking in at the Children's Museum. "Now remember, don't say *anything,* not a word," our handler coached as we drew closer. "If a child asks you a question, just give him a hug or something. Okay, we're about two feet from the platform. Excuse me, boys and girls, Ernie and Bert need some room to get through!" I was aware of the sensation of wading through small bodies, but all I could see were mothers, grimacing with false excitement and/or extreme irritation. The racket the kids were making reached me like the roar of the ocean heard in a seashell. I tried to remain calm, taking yoga breaths so I wouldn't hyperventilate inside my giant head. What if I passed out from lack of oxygen? I dearly wished the licensing people over at the Children's Television Workshop had let Bert wear regular old tennis shoes. Walking in those squashy high-tops was like navigating the surface of a marshmallow planet . . . on acid.

The department-store woman abruptly let go of my hand and turned to face the crowd. "Does anybody here like *Sesame Street?*" she screamed. The children and their mothers howled in the affirmative. Several startled infants wailed in terror. Something that felt like a monkey's paw seized my thigh at crotch level. "Honey," the department-store woman cooed, "Bert's going to want to say hello to you, but you have to wait your turn." Whatever was gripping my leg was pried loose as an adult hand—presumably belonging to the department-store woman—spun me around by the shoulder and propelled me toward the stage. I immediately barked my shins on the edge of the platform and pitched forward, dislocating my missile-shaped head on the folding chair that was to be my throne. Given the bumping and thrashing to my left, I deduced that Nate was having similar trouble. The department-store woman yanked Bert's head back into alignment and got me into the folding chair, where I sat, waving like an ignoramus, until Ernie had been dragged into position beside me.

For the first dozen kids or so, I worked hard to channel the spirit of Bert. I didn't want to destroy anyone's illusions, though it was kind of depressing how readily the little tykes accepted as the real thing an overgrown, mute impostor who avoided answering their questions by patting them in what he hoped appeared to be a kindly, nonlecherous manner. Many of them had brought along *Sesame Street* dolls. I couldn't help noticing that the Ernies far outnumbered the Berts. In fact, I got the distinct impression that some of these kids only deigned to sit on my lap because Ernie's was occupied. Nate was eating it up. I could hear him attempting Ernie's signature snicker and humming that rubber ducky song.

"Remember what we said about talking, 'Ernie,'" the department-store woman chirped threateningly.

Chastened, Nate reverted to patting and waving.

"Pick up the pace," the department-store woman hissed, her face pressed against the mesh panel in Bert's throat. We tried to step up the assembly line but failed miserably, thanks to the universal parental impulse to photograph their young. I could count on four fingers the number of children whose mothers had made this pilgrimage sans camera. Having waited hours to capture the moment, the paparazzi moms would be damned if they'd see their children leave our laps before they'd fired off enough shots to satisfy themselves that a winner lurked somewhere in the batch. By and large, the subjects seemed ready to call it quits long before the photographers. "Smile," the mothers hectored. "If you want that Orange Julius Mommy promised you, you'll pull that tongue back in your mouth and smile, Mister!" For the first half hour, I too smiled on command, but as the muscles surrounding my temporal mandibular joint started to seize up, it occurred to me that I could assume any expression I felt like and no one would be the wiser. Good thing Shaggy and Scooby weren't around to unmask me. After playing around with a variety of psychotic leers, I realized that I'd better buckle down and protect my eyes from all those automatic flashes. The mesh absorbed some of the ocular shock, but who was I to say that all those strobes wouldn't bring on a seizure of some kind?

"Is it okay if I take a picture, Bert?" a diaper-bag-toting mommy shouted as she cradled her infant in the crook of her arm.

I nodded my head by rocking back and forth at the waist, wondering what she planned to do with this solo shot. Paste it into the baby book as proof that the great and powerful Bert had once deigned to visit the mall near their home? "Timmy, you don't remember because you were just a baby, but look, there's Bert and see, the very same platform Santa sits on when he comes to Penney's!"

Without warning, she thrust the infant into my arms. To say I was ill prepared to receive this bundle grossly understates the situation. I hadn't held anyone that small since high school, when the neighbors, reassured by the presence of my mother right next door, had indulged my desire to earn a dollar an hour baby-sitting. The giant felt-and-papier-mâché Bert head obscuring my vision did nothing to make me feel more confident that I would remember how. Equine in its ability to sense fear, the baby started to shriek and buck, twisting its muscular torso in its mad desire to get free of the monstrous creature who had taken it from its mother. It was like trying to haul a healthy young sea bass into a rowboat with my bare hands. Actually, bare hands would have come in handy right about then. The accuracy of my Muppet gloves put me at a distinct disadvantage for going the distance with that thrashing mass of fragile human tissue. As the horrifying possibility of the baby torquing itself loose of my grip seemed more and more likely, its mother fumbled with her Instamatic. "Oh, darn it, I forgot to turn the flash on," she cursed.

"Pleasepleasepleaseplease," I whimpered inside Bert's cranium, as I struggled to keep the baby from doing a triple gainer. Unable to see the increasingly desperate little creature pushing against my lap with all its might, I kept my eyes fastened on the mother's camera.

"Oh, come on, you, turn on," she chided, addressing the small indicator light beside the viewfinder.

Oh my god, her batteries were low. "Turnonturnon-turnon," I begged. "I can't hold on much longer!" Where was the department-store woman? Couldn't anyone see that I was in trouble? Or that this baby had zero interest in getting its picture taken?

I wonder how many minutes that episode shaved off my life, as I waited for the light on the back of Mommy's camera to glow orange. Finally, she held the camera up to her eye, snapped the shutter, and then frowned. "Did the flash go off?" she asked uncertainly. Palming the baby, I davened frantically, praying that no one in the crowd would dare contradict Bert.

The baby sapped my energy so badly, I was unable to appreciate the one hardcore Bert fan to cross my lap. He was a little older than the others and chattered on about Ernie's and my twin beds and Mr. Hooper and I don't know what the fuck else. He showed me a long length of paper clips he had hooked together. I patted his thigh absentmindedly. "Wrap it up," the department-store woman mouthed, twirling her index finger in exasperation. I tried to hand the kid off to Nate, but he returned, paper clips in hand. "He brought that for you, Bert," his mother stressed, her expression conveying that management would most certainly be hearing from her. Given the baby, the pesky exhortations of the department-store woman, and my inability to swab the sweat from my eyes, nothing would have felt better than knocking that nasty mother down by butting her square in the chest with my pointy Bert head, but instead I writhed my way through all sorts of hokey mimed gestures. For me? Really? Paper clips? My heart's beating like a captured sparrow! I love you! I love you some more! "Just put it by his feet, Jason," the boy's mother scowled when it became clear that the big mustard dummy lacked the manual dexterity to pick up the gift. Only later did Nate tell me that Bert collects paper clips, a trait that must have eluded me when I was a regular viewer between the ages of three and six. And I never was part of the college gang that liked to fire up the bong and sing along with Big Bird every afternoon.

We'd been processing kids for well over the stipulated two hours, and still the line snaked back into Menswear. Nate's agency hadn't mentioned anything about overtime when they'd hooked us up with the gig. The department-store lady was losing what little cool she'd had to begin with and began barking things like "Time's up, sweetheart!" and "Decide which one's your favorite, because you can't sit on them both." This last edict was repealed when it resulted in a stampede toward Nate. So help him if he gloated about it when we got home. "Uh-uh, sorry, the new rule is, you sit on whoever's lap becomes available first," the department-store woman snapped, hoisting a blubbering Ernie fan onto my thighs. Mercifully, this arbitrary legislation was amended almost immediately. I didn't think I could take that many crying kids when, with every passing minute, the oxygen in my cranial chamber seemed less and less likely to sustain life.

"Boys and girls, Ernie and Bert have to go back to Sesame Street now." An outraged gasp from the mothers made me question the sanity of this decision. What if the angry mob tried to prevent us from leaving? It would be like that scene in *To Kill a Mockingbird* where a terrified Scout blunders through the woods as best she can, her progress grossly impeded by her papier-mâché ham costume. How would I ever find the storeroom? Maybe better to head toward the light. If I could make it to the parking lot, I could ditch my Bert gear behind the van and become just another shoeless shopper in mustard-colored 'tard and tights.

"Oh, all right!" the department-store woman conceded, as mutiny threatened. "They'll come down the line and shake hands, but *that's all!"* As a bottom-rung actor, I'd never been able to muster much in the way of sympathy for celebrities who bitched about the hardships of public adoration, but running the low-speed gauntlet past all those grasping *Sesame Street* devotees and their pissed-off moms changed all that. The department-store woman was hustling us along way faster than was prudent. Nate and I kept falling down on top of each other, ending up in the sort of bend-over-boyfriend sprawl the Children's Television Workshop takes pains never to depict.

There were cries of dismay as the familiar strains of *Sesame Street's* opening theme issued from the PA, signaling the event's conclusion. Waving in a sort of general farewell, we waded through the racks of tiny coordinates, the department-store woman blocking the groupies. I couldn't be sure, given the mesh, but I think she was zigzagging us back to the storeroom along an alternate route, the same tactic State Department employees use to avoid ambush. It didn't work. A mother lay in wait behind a pedestal full of mannequins, camera drawn. "My child has been waiting for hours to have his picture taken with them," she fumed. "How dare you cut the line before his turn?"

"Ma'am," the department-store woman countered in a tone more martial than customer service oriented, "There were more than a hundred people in that line, and I'm afraid Ernie and Bert have a very full schedule today. Isn't that right, Ernie?" Nate rocked from side to side like a dancing bear.

"What kind of people are you to disappoint a child like that," the mother spat. "You'll never see another cent of my business, do you hear? Baby, turn around so Mommy can get a picture of you with Ernie and Bert!"

"Ma'am, I'm afraid I can't let you do that. It wouldn't be fair to the others who waited in line—"

"Fair! You talk to me about *fair?*"

As the combatants faced off, I felt a pair of small arms encircling my waist. By arching my back and forcefully tucking in my chin, I was just barely able to get their owner in my sights. Untouched by the fury that consumed his mother, he gazed up with the radiant expression of those little kids flocking around Jesus in illustrated volumes of children's Bible tales. "I love you, Buwt," he announced, contentedly burying his nose in my foam rubber. Oh, suffer the little children to come unto me. What a little lamb, inadvertently absolving me of guilt for the photo his mother would not be permitted to take.

What was wrong with him that he didn't prefer Ernie?

screaming orgasms all around

Once Myra the Shot Girl had punched in for the night, I couldn't move a drink for love or money. When I approached the tables to suggest another round, recognition drained from the eyes of the customers who'd driven in from the outer 'burbs for an alcohol-soaked night on the town. These aging frat boys had done the math and realized that while a tray full of Kamikaze shots was fun, a round of Kamikaze shots purchased directly from Myra the Shot Girl was really, really fun. We all knew the score.

Doug, the manager, insisted that increasing sales was just a matter of trying harder. "Take my order," he told me, settling his meaty, chino-clad hams on a chair whose hideousness can only be described as bentwood reincarnated as chrome.

"What?"

"Take my order! I'm a customer. If you don't take my order soon, I may get sick of waiting around. I may go get my own drink from the bar, and I've got some news for you: If I do that once, I'm going to be doing that all night long." He smiled triumphantly. "Go ahead. Take my order."

"Would you like something to drink?" I played along, none too happily. Four years of theater school for this.

"Nope," he simpered, crossing his arms in front of his chest. I suppressed the urge to garrote him with the skinny necktie that hung like a plumb line on the vast tundra of his Big & Tall shop oxford shirt. "Try again."

"Hi, can I get you something from the bar?"

"Wrong! Here, give me your tray. You take the chair." Willing myself blind to the other staffers observing this charade from their opening stations, I did as instructed. Doug took a few paces back to prepare himself, then sashayed up to the table, my cork-bottomed tray held high on his tented fingers. "Hey guys, welcome to Clubland," he roared to me and my imaginary companions. "My name's . . ." He was pretending to be me, but he couldn't remember my name. His eyes shifted guiltily to the giant video monitors flanking the nearby stage, as if he hoped to find the answer flashing there. ". . . Raquelle, and I'll be your waitress tonight! Are you stoked to have fun tonight or what? So c'mon, what are we waiting for, let's get you fixed up with some drinks! Have you guys ever had a Screaming Orgasm?" I regarded him sourly. "Okay, Screaming Orgasms all around! In fact, I'll tell you what: It's going to get really crazy in here in a minute, so what I recommend is, why don't you order your second round right now, just in case I get stuck on the other side of the room? Sound good?" Hand on hip, he paused, beaming for a few seconds before dropping character to resume his managerial role. "See the difference in approach?"

"Mmm-hmm," I mumbled, digging at the beery carpet with the toe of my scuffed Converse All-Star, the only vestige of my identity left me. The cost of my uniform—T-shirt, black denim jacket, matching black jeans—was being deducted from my paycheck. Both the jacket and the T-shirt were emblazoned with a peppermint-striped logo that so closely resembled the one belonging to the board game Candyland, if I were Hasbro, I'd have sued. The other waitresses wore this garb better, which is to say *tighter,* than I. Once, I had tried to customize the uniform with my favorite hat, a battered fedora nicked from my high school drama department's wardrobe, but Doug had made me take it off, saying it didn't fit with Clubland's sophisticated, sexy image. For the rest of the evening, I attempted to hustle drinks with a sophisticated, sexy case of hat head.

Myra the Shot Girl got to wear what she wanted. She had several extremely flattering black rubber minidresses that she liked to team with a visored leather-daddy cap, but my favorite of all her outfits was a skin-tight, sleeveless, orange-wool catsuit that looked like the things I used to see in my mother's Swedish knitting magazines in the early 1970s. A bandolier of disposable shot glasses crossed her zeppelin-like bosom, and a wide belt slung low on her hips held bottles of Kool-Aid-colored shooters. My father would have been horrified. He was very strict when it came to alcohol and, early on, had laid down a bunch of commandments that, even now, I find difficult to disobey:

- Never ruin good liquor by mixing it with Coca-Cola.
- Stay away from sweet drinks because those are what give you the hangover.
- Pick one cocktail and stick to it all night.

- Mingling different kinds of booze is what makes you sick.

(He also has a story about falling off the kitchen counter when he was seven after taking a big swig from a bottle that smelled like oranges.)

Clubland's patrons fell off the counter left and right after Myra had been working the crowd for an hour or so. The beefier they were, the more her watermelons seemed to affect them. I was no stranger to public drunkenness. I had been to college, after all, and had even worked in a bar before, a real dive on the far North Side, where I'd once served B. B. King a 7-Up and he'd responded, "Thank you, baby, that tastes so nice." Biddy's was a pit, but I'd made money hand over fist there because it was reliably jam-packed with blues fans and I was one of only two cocktail waitresses working the joint. My sole coworker, hired the same day I was, was impregnated by the bartender before our first paychecks could be cut. They immediately quit to get married. I'm sure they're very happy. (My goodness, by now their child must be the same age I was when I worked with her parents—two years below the legal drinking limit.)

Biddy's was an ideal situation for a cocktail waitress whose customers behaved badly. It was so crowded that I could rarely get close to the people I was serving, meaning that the people over whose heads I was passing drinks were the ones who took the hit when somebody puked. If someone failed to tip me, she could jolly well fight her own way to the bar for the rest of the night. Knowing that the bartenders' professional code requires them to serve waitresses before customers, I would swing by the waitress station every time I noticed the chiseler waving a fistful of greenbacks. If somebody gave me exceptional 'tude, I could cruise up behind him when he was inching his way to the boggy bathroom and pinch his triceps as hard as I could. By the time he managed to turn around in that mob, I'd be long gone, my tray held high above the sea of heads like the dorsal fin of a shark.

Clubland was a nightclub of an entirely different stripe from gritty old Biddy's. For starters, it was so damn big that on our rare busy nights there was still room to circulate, so I couldn't pinch. Even on weeknights we were overstaffed, with no fewer than six waitresses on the floor. As the newest hire—and, let's not forget, least "sexy" and "sophisticated"—I was assigned to patrol the arid back section, far from the stage where the Clubland dancers gyrated. Decidedly unexotic, they reminded me of the modern dance troupe at my college, the girls all former gymnasts, the boys all moussed self-importance, even when garbed in fuchsia harem pants. They appeared at regular intervals, their choreographed routines enhanced by swirling pink and orange amoebas projected on the video screens. The goth kids who frequented the underage club on the other side of the El platform would have made mincemeat out of them, but our customers tended to watch them with a sort of bovine tolerance, if not any real appreciation or enthusiasm. Perhaps they accepted watered-down modern dance as just part of the big-night-in-the-big-city package, along with coat-check service and gay guys walking down the sidewalk hand in hand.

I had a chip on my shoulder about the clientele Clubland attracted. I suspected they were the sort of people who enjoyed eating at Bennigan's, and when I was a sophomore in college, the Bennigan's interviewer had refused to hire me because I had "two-tone" hair, which, like nose rings and beards, projected an image at odds with the restaurant's corporate standards. It was a bit of an anarchist thrill to fall short of such square criteria. For a few days I traipsed around campus recounting the incident and debating whether the ACLU should get involved. I clearly didn't learn my lesson, though, or I wouldn't have been working for and serving cocktails to people like Doug, i.e., people who might believe dining at Bennigan's was every bit the crazy fun Bennigan's advertising jingles insisted. People I suspected of admiring the papier-mâché unicorn heads mounted like hunting trophies in the stairwells leading up to the balcony and down to the bathrooms. People who thought the candy-cane-striped play-on-words name was *clever.*

Disliking the customers is an even greater bummer when one's chance at financial reward from their inebriation evaporates at 11:30 PM, the hour when Myra the Shot Girl made her appearance. Because the usual turf rules didn't apply to her, I was able to observe her effect on the customers at close range. As she supplanted me tableside, I leaned on the brass rail dividing the tiers, smiling self-consciously, not that the dunderheads horking down her wares were the slightest bit inclined to notice me. The way they imbibed Peach Kamikaze rounds closely mimicked the six stages of death. First came Gaiety: the sheer pleasure of having someone who looked like Octopussy pouring specimen cups of brightly colored liquid for you and all your buddies. Next was Gaiety-with-an-Edge, the sort of reckless high spirits that ensure every question that can be answered with a polite "yes" is instead met with a resounding "fuck, yeah!" The third stage, Braggadocio, involved top-volume claims of outrageous party animality bestowed on either oneself or the fattest, shyest member of the group. This deteriorated into Squishy Sentimentality, the stage in which acquaintances from work were transformed into *besht* friends, a connection that outlasted the pumpkin's reign as Cinderella's coach by mere minutes. "You guys are so sweet," Myra purred without betraying the slightest disgust, the fantasy baby sitter who combined genuine warmth with impossible hotness. Fumbling through their wallets, mumbling about how trashed they were, the shot drinkers actually trumped death by reaching Acceptance at round five. This freed up round six to be all about Getting John to The Bathroom Before He Fucking Heaves.

If you're keeping score, that's fifteen ounces of vodka, Triple Sec, and god knows what in ten minutes, with Myra collecting something in the neighborhood of forty smackers per head while I stood idly by. I should note that the merrymakers were not exclusively male. Bachelorette parties were, if anything, raunchier, rowdier, and more likely to progress to a seventh round. Transactions with the Shot Girl were certain to juice up the sexual current running through mixed-gender groups. (Clubland lacked the freewheeling amyl-nitrate energy that might have made it worth a gay man's while to venture several blocks from the nearby Boys Town bar scene.) The whiff of Weimar Berlin, or at least the film version of *Cabaret,* hung about Myra. Who knows, under different circumstances, I too might have been tempted to buy what she was selling. Unfortunately, when she worked my turf, the only sales I could hope for were the party-pooping screwdrivers ordered by sour girlfriends, resentful that their men were lavishing so much attention and money on a goddess with whom no frizz-banged, heart-locketed fiancée could compete. "Ayun, do you think you could . . ." Myra—who was not supposed to waste her time running back and forth to the bar for regular drink orders—would venture, twiddling the bow tie of cash clamped between her second and third fingers. I appreciated the humility with which she asked, particularly on those nights when she'd accessorized with a bullwhip. In return for expediting, I received a smile that was all the more dazzling for its sincerity and a tip that exceeded the one she'd been given for that entire round. Yeah, Myra the Shot Girl was okay in my book.

"I called you all together like this because I consider each and every one of you a part of the Clubland family," Doug began his mandatory all-staff meeting, as a prelude to berating us for a variety of misdeeds—everything from garnishing Rum and Cokes with maraschino cherries instead of limes (guilty!) to inadequately pushing the sporting event–style food menu he'd recently added. Again, guilty. What kind of "sexy and sophisticated" nightclub trucks in microwaved Velveeta nachos? What kind of "family" makes you pay for your uniform out of your wages? Besides, Clubland had been open for only a couple of months, more than ample time for my former Biddy's coworkers to get cracking on a baby, true, but hardly long enough to forge what I would consider strong familial bonds. Why, only that summer, I had ridden my bike down Belmont, past the long-shuttered movie palace in which we now sat, and daydreamed about what it must have been like in its heyday. What I couldn't do with a space like that, I had thought, though in all my wild imaginings it had never once occurred to me to rip out the seats, replace the screen with a bank of video monitors and a cheesy *Flashdance*-inspired catwalk for an in-house modern dance troupe, and rechristen the grand old structure with the stupidest name I could possibly come up with. Sometimes, when my section was doornail dead or I'd suffered through a pinch-worthy affront with no possible recourse, I'd wander to the balcony, where vestiges of the building's former glory remained untouched. "I'm so sorry for what they've done to you," I'd whisper, patting the ancient stucco wall. I took its silence for complicity. It, too, found the insipid candy-cane logo demeaning. It would have let me keep the fedora. Left to its druthers, the Old Vic would have kept its original name, reinventing itself not as some cheezoid nightspot, but as a desiccated, ghostly-cool performance-art venue, or better yet, a revival house showing the exact same films it had in its heyday. Yeah, those old walls were in my corner. Had they been in bed with management, they would have started bellowing, "Hey, welcome to Clubland! You look like you're up for some serious partying! Can we get you rolling with some Sex On The Beach?"

"All it takes is a little commitment on your part," Doug droned on, pressing his mandatory meeting point. "For instance, let's say that Ziggy here has just ordered a round of drinks." He gestured toward the rockabilly barback, who cringed, stricken at being singled out. "And I'm the waitress. 'Okay, sir, I'll be right back with those Long Island Iced Teas! But before I go, would you care to take advantage of our new food service? People who are dancing and partying and having a good time get hunnnnnnngry! Am I right? We've got pizza, hot dogs, nachos . . . oh, is that your stomach growling? No, I'm just kidding you! Seriously, though, how about a round of hot dogs with your drinks'?"

"Okay," Ziggy whispered, staring at the cocktail napkin he had twisted into something resembling a corn-husk doll.

"See how easy that was, people?" Doug demanded, hitching his khakis back to their starting position, just shy of his spherical abdomen's equator. Someone behind me snorted. I detected a momentary expression of panic on Doug's face before his eyebrows rose in a classic attitude of teacherly exasperation. "Carmelita, do you have something you'd like to share with the group?"

I rubbernecked as discreetly as possible. Carmelita sat smoking Merit Ultra Lights in the back row, her stiletto-heeled booties kicked up on the brass rail, her chair tilted so far back it was a miracle she didn't tip over and bang her ink-colored cockscomb on the carpeted cement stairs leading to the bar. Doug awaited her reply, fists on hips. Smirking, she shook her head as she expelled a mentholated plume through her nostrils.

"Please, Carmelita, I think we'd all be interested to learn just what it is you find so funny." Doug seized his braided belt, winching his pants into place again, a gesture that failed to establish the upper hand.

"That's okay," Carmelita shot back, winking at one of her bartender cronies as she picked a shred of tobacco from her teeth. Given my feelings toward authority figures in general and Doug in particular, the natural assumption is that I would root for Carmelita, my fellow cocktail waitress, to emerge the victor from this verbal joust. However, Carmelita had scared the stuffing out of me from day one and seemed to take a grim, if largely incidental, pleasure in doing so. I didn't think it was personal, as there was no significant way in which I could matter to her. I wasn't out to steal her man. I didn't even know if she had a man, though once I overheard her discussing a mutual acquaintance with a male bartender, emphatically swearing that she'd cut that bitch's pussy off if the dumb whore ever tried to fuck with her again. The notion that this grudge was of a romantic nature is pure conjecture on my part. It could have been money related. When she wasn't hustling drinks, Carmelita kept up a running commentary on her seemingly innumerable debts. She owed money to her landlord, the old lady who took care of her kid, some guy who had sold her a piece-of-shit guitar, her tattoo artist, and someone named Jimmy, who was apparently an honorary member of a core group of Clubland post-shift binge drinkers. Maybe Jimmy was her man. Whoever he was, he was getting sick of waiting for the two hundred bucks she still owed him for a really nice pool table with tassels and shit on the corners.

"Carmelita, what the fuck do you want that pool table for?" one of the bartenders growled affectionately as we wiped down tables and bused the final glasses back at night's end. "All you ever do is pass out on it."

"You can suck my dick, faggot," Carmelita parried, playfully splashing the dregs of an abandoned cocktail in the vicinity of her friend's face.

"Anytime, doll." On her way back to collect another tray full of dead soldiers, Carmelita pulled up the hem of her T-shirt, flashing him one of her apple-hard, bare-naked titties. I couldn't tell if their interaction constituted a form of gender-blind locker-room banter or a carny courtship ritual. Several of the other waitresses hooted with approval as Carmelita sauntered away. "What are you looking at," she challenged, narrowing her heavily penciled eyes as we passed.

"Nothing," I chirped, scuttling away, suddenly ashamed of my bra, which now struck me as babyish, so cottony and white it might as well have been held together with diaper pins. There was no telling what Carmelita, seething with barely controlled, post-shift, about-to-get-wasted energy, might do. She might knock me down and strip me! I had recently read an article in one of the alternative weeklies about the brutal hazing rites of a local street gang's ladies' auxiliary. It wasn't a stretch to imagine Carmelita jumping someone in, laughing raucously in her snug, side-laced skank pants as the abused novice blubbered at her feet, nude save for a thick white-cotton brassiere. Prudence dictated I steer clear of her.

I spent Christmas Eve in Indiana with my father, but the night before that I spent at Clubland. The place was so deserted, even Myra couldn't make a go of it. Doug had arranged for *It's a Wonderful Life* to play on the giant video screens, and after a while, the DJ was instructed to cease and desist so we could enjoy the film with its original soundtrack. The bartenders came out from behind the bar, joining the cocktail waitresses at the tables as the dancers sat cross-legged on the stage, staring up like mesmerized tots. Apparently, Carmelita was the only employee who had never seen this Yuletide chestnut. She sat with a couple of her cronies, chomping intently on the stem of a cherry from her Tequila Sunrise, her eyes glued to the screen. When all the characters at last crowded into Jimmy Stewart's living room to pay off his bank debt, she abruptly stood up. "I'm sorry, but this is just total fucking bullshit," she announced. Looking at the dozens of giant Donna Reed heads misting up the screens, I found myself in total agreement.

On New Year's Eve, I was demoted to cork-puller and was positioned out in the lobby beside several barrels full of cheap champagne bottles. On the street, the bouncers were wearing ski masks. Revelers limped in with snowdrifts in their stiff coiffures, the females' legs bare under puffy Michelin Man parkas. Doug in his tuxedo looked very much like the inept lackey Robert DeNiro beats to death with a baseball bat in *The Untouchables*. Every few minutes, he'd run into the lobby to announce the number of minutes remaining in the year. I wondered if I would be permitted into the nightclub proper to see the ball drop on the video screens. With almost two hours to go until midnight, I could no longer feel my fingers digging in the ice to lay claim to fresh bottles, which I then struggled to uncork without putting out any unsuspecting eyes. I'd been instructed to greet incoming customers with a complimentary plastic flute of sub-Andre, but most of them wrinkled their noses at the offer. Several fellows joked that they'd take a hot coffee instead, and, conditioned to behave in such a way as to encourage tipping, I laughed like I'd never before encountered such sharpness of spontaneous wit. Then they'd go in through the big double doors, and I'd be left shivering beside the former ticket booth in nothing but my almost-paid-for denim outfit, chewing over the shortcomings of 1988 as I watched their slushy footprints dissolve in dirty puddles on the tile floor. I was beginning to feel a bit necrotic, but then I discovered that cheap champagne warmed the body as well as the spirit. The next time one of the bouncers stamped in, seeking brief respite from the windchill in the not-much-discernibly-warmer lobby, I slipped him a bottle. Grinning, he headed back outside. Ten minutes later, he came back to return his empty. "I'm sorry, I forgot your name . . ." he started.

Just then Doug burst through the doors with his compulsive time update. "What are you doing in here?" he asked, frowning at my bouncer friend, beside whom Doug looked almost dainty, the way a 48-ounce convenience-store soda cup shrinks in contrast to the 64-ouncers stacked alongside.

"C'mon, man, it's like minus twenty out there," the bouncer complained, removing his ski gloves to blow on his hands.

"This is nothing," Doug scoffed. "Just be glad we're closed tomorrow. Weather report says it's going to feel like forty below with the windchill. Don't let me catch you in here again." We waited until the door swung shut behind him. Above the strains of "Louie Louie," I could hear a female voice screeching, "Oh my god, I'm *so* drunk!"

"Technically, isn't it tomorrow in about an hour and fifteen minutes?" I mused, digging my frostbitten claw into the ice barrel.

The bouncer smiled, pulling his ski mask down from his forehead. "Anyway, I just came in to say thanks. It did a lot to warm us guys up out there."

"Anytime. Happy New Year. Have another. Have two." It wasn't so much pilfering as ending the year on an auspicious note, easing the burden of a fellow toiler, who returned to his arctic post with two full bottles nestled like extra lungs underneath his down filling. I could tell he was sharing with the other two moose-sized men on the job, because every so often they'd wave to get my attention long enough to give me a thumbs-up through the glass doors. I'd have kept them supplied all night long, but with forty-five minutes until countdown, I was rotated back to the serving floor. Something about Carmelita being too lit to keep up with customer demand. Even though the move was sanctioned, I was apprehensive about how she'd react to splitting her section with me. I needn't have worried. Whatever she'd been swilling from the bottomless coffee cup stashed next to the olives and lemon twists obviously agreed with her. "Fuck this stupid bitch of a year," she screamed, slinging a comradely arm around my neck. "If I go into the tech booth to smoke a bowl with the sound guy, you're gonna cover for me, right?"

"Of course," I bellowed, positioning my mouth right up against her ear. "Take all the time you need!"

"Love you, baby," she screeched.

With Carmelita out of the picture, there was serious dough for the taking. The holiday had quadrupled the customer population. The dance floor was packed, the aisles were impassable, and the temperature was so hot and humid, I started having a claustrophobic reaction to my black jeans. Clubgoers in wilting finery crowded around me, shrieking simultaneous slurred drink orders. "Two Michelob, Stoli on the rocks, three Long Islands, Coke no ice, Irish coffee, gin and tonic, vodka tonic, gin and 7, vodka cranberry, four Bloody Marys, one plain tomato juice," I gabbled, struggling to keep multiple orders in my head long enough to reach the waitress station.

"Miss! Excuse me, Miss! Do you know what happened to the other waitress, kind of petite with a big panther tattoo?"

"Two Michelob, Stoli on the rocks, three Long Islands,

Coke no ice, Irish coffee, gin and tonic, vodka tonic, gin and 7, vodka cranberry, four Bloody Marys, one plain tomato juice," I responded, trudging toward the bar, determined not to let the man hanging onto my elbow erase my mantra. The bartender would ream me a new cornhole when I delivered my long list in the order it was received instead of rearranging it so that liquors of a certain species were grouped together, with top shelves leading and soft drinks bringing up the rear—but so be it.

"Because she was supposed to bring us a margarita, two Jack and Cokes, a Fuzzy—"

"Two Michelob, Stoli on the rocks, three Long Islands, Coke no ice, Irish coffee, gin and tonic, vodka tonic, gin and . . . and . . . " Poof. Just like that. Gone. I whirled angrily on the jacket-holder but suddenly realized that even if I'd managed to deliver my baroque tally word for word, I wouldn't have recognized the people who'd placed the orders, and the crowd was so amorphous that the odds of finding them in the spots where I'd left them were nil at best. I took a good look at the patron who'd derailed my train of thought. Red hair, wire-rim specs, vomitrocious sweater his mother had given him for Christmas, the beginnings of a pimple between his eyes. "Okay, tell me your order one more time and then don't move."

In the time it took to fight my way to the bar—margarita, two Jack and Cokes, Fuzzy Navel, pimple between the eyes—I considered my position. The customers paid for their drinks when they were delivered, not when they ordered them. Before the bartenders would let us take our trays, we had to cover the full cost of the customers' drinks from the "banks" of cash we carried tucked between our fingers. Every shift, there was some misunderstanding that led to a waitress eating somewhere between ten and forty dollars' worth of drinks. Maybe a drunken customer had double-ordered with two different waitresses, or a party had decided that what they really wanted to do was go home. There were any number of recipes for getting stuck with the chit, but the last night of the year seemed rife with opportunities to get boned. I could feel the stress building, the way it used to in school when all my final projects were due on the same day. Thirsty customers shouted and flailed in vain. I might as well have been a taxi with my meter off.

"Where the fuck's Carmelita?" the bartender roared as I finally pulled into the station.

"Getting high in the sound booth, margarita, two Jack and Cokes, Fuzzy Navel," I screamed, seizing a fistful of lime wedges and little red cocktail straws. We were all going to wake up with laryngitis at this rate. "Oh, and eight bottles of Heineken!"

As I made my way back to the obedient Mr. Pimple Head, I unloaded every bottle on my tray, each at a one-dollar markup. When customers tried to get me to fetch them a cocktail or a soda or, most egregious of all, a free glass of tap water, I shook my head. "Sorry, I'm just the Beer Girl! You want some beer? Ice-cold beer here!" I developed a patter not unlike the entrepreneurs who illegally drag Hefty bags of supermarket-purchased refreshments through the public parks. "No wait! Ice-cold Heinies! Who's next?" I was thronged. Even without Myra's black rubber getup and everything that went beneath it, I felt like a star.

Shortly before midnight, I ran into Doug, wiping the sweat from his beet-red brow with a cocktail napkin. He asked me if I was having a good night. Less than two hours later, after a run-in with a customer whose strapless acetate mini had gotten caught in a Heineken shower when she bumped me on the dance floor, I would be in his office, turning in my almost-paid-for uniform and arranging where to have my final paycheck sent. For now, though, I was the life of the party, a high-earning member of the Clubland family, Ayunee the Mercenary Beer Girl, and I was having one hell of a good night.

in the weeds

When I landed a job at Dave's Italian Kitchen, I felt like I'd hit the big time. I'd been running through restaurants at an alarming rate, but I still wasn't a very good waitress. I was slow, I couldn't carry more than three plates at a time, and when one of my orders got fucked up, I tended to hide in the bathroom even if the fault lay with the cooks (which it rarely did). I had yet to don a food-service uniform that improved upon the loathsome duds required by the Children's Museum or Clubland. I expressed my sartorial objections by rarely washing my apron or the dumpy black pants I was inevitably expected to wear with a white shirt and a tie. I always smelled like salad dressing. My entire life, I have hated salad dressing, even on salad. Although I would make an attempt to pull my long hair back into a hygienic ponytail, several lank strands always managed to escape, dangling into my eyes and, occasionally, my mouth. This was later regarded as a charming character detail when I posed nude for a figure-drawing class, but it infuriated restaurant honchos. One pompous pre-Dave's prick rode me mercilessly about my inability to control my "slovenly" hair. It's a miracle he never tried to give me bangs with a pair of kitchen shears.

That place, Palucci's, was a real nightmare, an overpriced Italian bistro that sold gelato and cappuccino up front during the day. The prick's wife and several of her cronies appeared every lunchtime, laden with shopping bags from upscale boutiques, to hog the window table for hours. They ordered cappuccino, and if I failed to froth the milk to their specifications, they looked at me like I'd left a turd floating in their cups. Under the imperious gaze of Kitty Palucci and her well-heeled pals, I never could get that damn cappuccino machine's steamer to work properly. There was no incentive. They refrained from tipping, and although they saw me five afternoons a week, they never learned my name, preferring to refer to me as "that girl."

The day shift at Palucci's was pretty slow. Often my only other customer was Palucci's best friend, a commercial theater producer who availed himself of complimentary sundaes and my sub-par cappuccino. He knew I had majored in acting. I suspected that he was waiting for me to fall to my knees and genuflect before him, but in hindsight, this was pure emotional self-defense. He was, after all, a successful theatrical producer, and I was a sloppy-looking, under-ambitious twenty-three-year-old actress, unwilling to wear makeup or drop the fifteen pounds I couldn't believe I needed to lose before anyone would be willing to send me out on commercial auditions. I consoled myself that this fat cat, who observed Kitty's rule of thumb that a 15 percent gratuity of zero is zero, produced crowd-pleasing schlock like *Steel Magnolias.* In the richly appointed theater of my mind, I starred in the complete works of Shakespeare and Chekhov. In reality, I lurked near the cappuccino machine, glowering behind unruly strands of hair at those I was fated to serve. Every so often, I ducked below the counter to sneak spoonfuls of gelato, egged on by my fellow waitress and aspiring actress, Shawna.

Shawna was a diabetic whom I indulged much as Laura Ingalls Wilder indulged her blind sister Mary when she described the sights taken in with her own healthy eyes. When it came to gelato, I was Shawna's mouth.

"Hmm, pistachio. I wonder what that would taste like," Shawna would muse, handing me a tasting spoon loaded with three times the amount we were supposed to offer customers.

"Don't you want me to try some of the crème brûlée?" I'd ask, greedily helping myself to another bite.

"*Ooh,* no! It looks like phlegm!" Shawna would reply, loud enough for the customers to hear.

Dave's Italian Kitchen didn't have gelato, but that was its only drawback compared with Palucci's or any of the other twenty-plus restaurants I had worked in—some for no more than a day. For starters, there was the extremely flexible dress code, which Dave had implemented only after repeated customer complaints. The dress code was this: no cutoffs and no bikini tops worn in lieu of shirts. That was it. Once, years later, a new acquaintance was trying to figure out why I looked so familiar. When it came out that she lived in the vicinity of Dave's, I told her that I had worked there for a couple of years. "Oh, Dave's Italian Kitchen!" she laughed. "My husband won't go there. He calls it the place with all the braless waitresses."

You'd think a straight man would dig his proximity to a

neighborhood institution whose waitresses eschew bras, but then, Dave's was no Hooters. The spaghetti carbonara was light years better, and furthermore, I know I always wore a bra, albeit a loose, ineffectual one, under my sleeveless thrift-store frocks. What I didn't do was shave my armpits, and Dave never said a word about it. To this day, he's the best boss I ever had.

Most food-service brass consider even the tiniest fuck-up sufficient reason to stage a giant public stink. Not Dave. Unlike other sadists in whose kitchens I've had the displeasure of toiling, Dave bypassed every opportunity to pump himself up by screaming at an employee who'd undercharged a party of ten or pissed off a table by dropping the entrées they'd been waiting for ever since a certain somebody forgot to turn in their ticket to the cooks an hour ago. If he thought my forelock amiss, he didn't mention it. Apparently, he was confident that we would learn from our mistakes, although more than once he inadvertently set me up to make more of them by disrupting my rhythm—which was already syncopated at best. With every table in my section filled, I'd pinwheel around the kitchen, bumping into the more capable waitpersons, who appeared like magic to retrieve their orders the second the cooks summoned them. If someone had spilled a puddle of creamy garlic dressing on the tile floor and neglected to mop it up, I was a shoe-in to slip in it, jettisoning every plate I'd been carrying. While I was busy on my hands and knees picking up the shards, the host would seat me with three new tables. My entrées were coming up as I was ladling out bowls of the minestrone that had been ordered as a first course. Waiters refer to this state as being "in the weeds." Dave seemed keenly attuned to the moment when the encroaching weeds threatened to devour the least skilled of his waitresses. That's when he would summon me over to the pizza ovens, which he manned in a T-shirt, shoveling pies in and out with a long-handled wooden paddle.

"Yeah, Dave, what is it?" I'd gabble, riffling through my green guest checks in a frenzy. I'd be practically panting. "My extra-large half-sausage half-mushroom can't be up yet, can it? I haven't even turned in the ticket. Shit. Sorry. I'm sort of losing it. Whoops, I just heard Jim ringing my bell! Four, that's me, right? I'm coming!"

Dave would lean his forearms on the counter and peek at me from between stainless-steel shelves filled with cooking utensils and industrial-sized shakers of oregano. "Hey, Buddy," he'd drawl in his resonant baritone, "I was just wondering . . . have you ever read any Evelyn Waugh?"

Dave was a good man. He was Jewish, not Italian—he had started the business twenty years earlier after a brief stint working for a restaurant supplier. He claimed he'd been appalled at the lengths to which most of the restaurant managers he supplied would go, using only the cheapest, nastiest ingredients to drive their profits up or, probably more accurately, stand a chance of breaking even. His experience confirmed what I had seen firsthand in my previous jobs. (One bit of wisdom I like to pass along to people who've never been backstage in a restaurant is: Never order anything that comes with glazed strawberries. I've been harping on this since high school, when I manned the dessert table at Herb's Deli. Of all the horrifying things I've seen in the workplace, pre-glazed strawberries rank near the top.) Dave harnessed his moral outrage at the food-service chicanery he'd witnessed when he opened his own restaurant, which turned out to be a gold mine. In college, I had steered clear of Economics, attracted by the siren song of Presentational Aesthetics. Dave's Italian Kitchen provided me with the basic Econ ed I had eluded for so long (not that I have ever managed to apply the sound business practices I learned there to my own life).

At the outset, Dave had shelled out for an industrial mixer and a pasta cutter, hulking metal contraptions that I feared the way I feared my grandmother's old-fashioned mangle, the one she said would take my arm off if I ventured too close. I was terrified that, skidding on a pat of butter that had tumbled unnoticed from a bread basket, I would pitch headfirst into the pasta cutter while it was busy pumping out a batch of spinach rotini, or "green noodles," as we called them. "GN" for short. Dave offered these GN and three other proletariat shapes of pasta together with several choices of high-cholesterol sauce for unbelievably modest prices. An enormous plate of spaghetti marinara was only $2.95. I rejoiced when every single person at a four-top ordered lasagna, because I'd be looking at a minimum tip of three dollars, assuming someone at the table knew how to calculate percentages.

Despite his rock-bottom prices, I always made a lot of moolah at Dave's. On a Saturday night in section 1 or 2, a hoary old vet like Gert or Judy could walk with two hundred fifty bucks easy. As the shift wore on, we stuffed our tips in ricotta buckets with our names scrawled across the side in magic marker. At the end of the night, we'd retire to the smoking section one by one to shake our ricotta buckets out over the red-and-white-checked oilcloths, eager to count our tips and check them against our section's share of the grand total. Rooting for 20 percent, I was satisfied with 15 but pissed if all those crumpled ones I'd been transferring from the dirty tabletops to my ricotta bucket amounted to anything less than that. We were expected to tip out 1 percent of our total food sales to the busboys, a much lower amount than is standard restaurant practice. Dave paid them far higher wages than they could have earned busing anywhere else. At the Kitchen, tipping out was a symbolic act, a show of respect to the guys who had busted their butts alongside us, hauling unappetizing dishpans and re-setting tables while people who'd been waiting in the lobby for twice the host's estimate breathed down their necks. At other places I'd worked, if you had a lousy night, your busboy did, too, as his cut was 15 percent of your tips, not 1 percent of however much cheapy-cheap rotini with butter and garlic you'd managed to move. Try handing a busboy seven dollars at the end of a long shift and see how much he loves you.

The busboys at Dave's were all Vietnamese. Many of them were ambitious high school boys who attended class all day and then worked until almost midnight. They all sought to emulate Ho, a star waiter who had risen up from their ranks. Ho was amazing. He never broke a sweat, no matter how many tables the host seated him with simultaneously. Not once did I encounter him in the weeds. He was soft spoken and neat. Compared to the braless partying waitresses, he was a miracle of discretion.

Outside of Ho, who was in a category by himself, there were essentially two tiers to the wait staff. There were the recent college grads like me, people in their early twenties with foolish, romantic degrees and a reasonable chance of knowing who Evelyn Waugh was or, if male, playing in a not-so-good rock band with Dave. We were seen as second-class citizens by the queen bees, Gert and Judy, and the rest of their crew, who, like the cooks, had started as teenagers right when the Kitchen first opened. They made the schedules and reported to Dave if someone needed to be fired. The no-bikini-top policy had been put in place in an effort to keep them within the bounds of decency. They ruled the roost, not always with Dave's grace or compassion. In all probability, his magnanimity was only possible because he ceded control of the more pugnacious tasks to these women, tough and loyal townies who weren't afraid to be bitchy. They were excellent waitresses. Manners-wise, they could never have cut it in fine dining, but for sheer ability to turn tables, keep their orders straight, and terrace plates right up their arms from wrist to pit, they couldn't be beat. They made money hand over fist, then ran through it fast. A couple of them were rumored to have impressive drug habits. One time when I asked a cook to help me unclog a drain in the bathroom, he told me to get Gert. "She'll take care of it for you. That nose of hers is like a fucking vacuum cleaner."

Besides the wait staff, the busboys, and the cooks, there was an odd assortment working their way down the ladder in other positions. There were hosts and bartenders, aspiring waiters whose job it was to sell 75-cent glasses of wine-in-a-box to the testy crowd in the small holding pen that passed for a lobby. Dave never advertised, but from the time the doors opened at 4:30 in the afternoon, the place was packed. The people waiting to be seated had a clear view past the host and bartender into the kitchen, where we nonveteran waiters sneaked bites of our customers' leftover chicken Marsala before wrapping the remaining portion to go. This gross violation of health codes made little sense, since Dave let us order practically anything we wanted from the menu for free. Chicken and veal dishes ran us four bucks. The only thing he asked us not to eat was the chocolate mousse, which was stored in a nonindustrial refrigerator at the back of the dining room, where the soda and coffee dispensers were. It was not uncommon for a customer searching for the john to stumble across a waitress crouched behind the refrigerator's open door, pile-driving chocolate mousse. We also suckled cannoli filling straight from the bag's teat, again in full view of the throng wedged into the tiny lobby.

I became very proud of my identity as a waitress once I no longer had to answer to Miss Thing, wear a sexless black-and-white uniform, and/or get stiffed frothing milk for the boss's wife. Dave's didn't even *have* a cappuccino machine, though we did have our share of troublesome customers. There was a repellent couple named, I swear to god, the Piggies. The Piggies had been eating at Dave's once a week since it opened, and of course they thought they owned the joint. Gert or Judy would greet them like royalty at the door, only to pawn them off immediately on me or the similarly low-ranking Isaac. This was a great disappointment to the Piggies, who knew about the hierarchy of the waiters. Isaac and I were artsy college kids. We wouldn't last more than a couple of years. Gert and Judy were there for the duration. The Piggies could be seated only at booth 6, a prime bit of real estate that could easily accommodate a large party of prime tippers who would eat and get out. The Piggies liked their food prepared in certain ways, depending on who was cooking that night. They'd detain me forever, forcing me to recite their order back to them, suspicious that a rookie would never be able to remember all their little nuances and pet peeves. I would try to smile reassuringly, which only seemed to aggravate them more. Meanwhile, I could hear the cooks pounding on the bell and roaring my name as orders I'd placed backed up along the counter.

One night Mrs. Piggie, tasting her manicotti, further puckered her sphincter-like lips. "I can't eat this. There's no way Jim cooked this. Take it back and tell them I want Jim to cook it." I carried the plate into the kitchen and told Jim, who had cooked it, what Mrs. Piggie had said. Jim, a taciturn, long-suffering man engaged to marry the perkiest of the veteran waitresses, rolled his eyes and shoved it back in the oven.

"She says she likes it brown on—"

"I know. I know. Brown on the edges, but not too brown, with just enough sauce, whatever that means. Fucking Piggies." Re-plating the manicotti, he sent me back to booth 6.

Without so much as a grunt of appreciation, Mrs. Piggie forked up a small bite, then yipped like a Yorkshire terrier. "No! This is all wrong! Did you tell Jim it's for me? Honestly!"

She flung herself back against the tall wooden booth, glaring at her husband with hostility, as if to say, "Well, what can you expect from these new people?" Uncorking a bottle of wine nearby, Isaac (soon to supplant Nate in my affections) gave me a sympathetic wink.

Back in the kitchen, Jim stonewalled, refusing to tinker any further with the manicotti or to prepare anything else for Mrs. Piggie to eat that evening. I pleaded, to no avail. Finally, one of the other cooks, a loose cannon named Tommy, reached across to snatch the plate from my hands. "Gimme that!" he shouted, throwing the manicotti into a hot pan with an entire stick of butter. After knocking it around with a wooden spoon for a couple of seconds, he spit into the pan and then re-plated the offending dish yet again, this time with a fresh ladle's worth of meat sauce. "There! Give that to the old bitch and make sure she eats every bite! Tell her that Jim cooked it!"

I did as instructed, and anyone who has ever worked in a restaurant will be glad—if hardly surprised—to learn that Mrs. Piggie cleaned her plate on this third attempt, cooing contentedly over the special treatment "Jim" had lavished on her.

The walls of Dave's Italian Kitchen were lined with testaments to the abiding power of love. Parties who finished a bottle of wine could autograph the dead soldier's label and ask their waiter to place this souvenir on the ledge that ran around the dining room just above eye level. There it would remain for eternity—or at least until another starry-eyed drunken couple sent their bottle up to replace it. Besides the fresh daisies on the red-and-white tablecloths and some terrifying abstract acrylics by a delivery guy who lived upstairs, the bottles were the only attempt at decoration in the place. It was another genius move on Dave's part, a way to ensure that he'd move some higher-ticket vino along with the stuff that flew out of the box for cheap.

Once, when the Bulls were winning the Superbowl or something of that magnitude was keeping the customers away, a fellow waitress named Drake-Ann (a bit of an anomaly, artsy, educated, but also partying and braless) and I amused ourselves by reading the dusty bottles, looking for the names of people we knew. I recognized lots of friends from college, sometimes wondering why I hadn't been invited to join the boisterous parties of six who'd preserved their Falstaffian merriment by signing the very vessels that had contained the mirth-making elixir. While I was thus ruminating, Drake-Ann fished her pen out of her apron and scrawled something on a bottle she had taken down.

"Drake-Ann, what are you doing?" I hissed, scandalized.

Flashing her engaging, irresponsible smile, she passed it over for my inspection. I squinted at the label:

> *Michael and Debbie got engaged at Dave's Italian Kitchen on April 14, 1982. Love you forever. P.S.—Drake-Ann was here too.*

I couldn't believe she had breached the sanctity of the bottles.

"Oh, stop being such a goody-goody! Who do you think ever looks at these old things?" she taunted, holding her pen up for me to take. Shaking my head, I glanced around to make sure we were unobserved. What would Gert say to Dave if she caught us at this asinine prank, horning in on other people's long-gone good times? Wanting to bond with Drake-Ann, I shrugged uneasily, then, feeling like a brat, added my two cents:

I was also here. Congratulations Mike + Debbie!
2 Sweet 2 B 4-gotten, Ayun Halliday.

We skipped around the dining room, embellishing bottles at random until we grew weary of the game.

Several weeks later, I saw a couple in my section take a bottle off the ledge and hold it up to the light. Uh-oh. I wished I'd never let Drake-Ann pressure me into that stupid stunt. What if I'd signed their special bottle, thinking I was so funny? What if they asked to speak to the manager? Racked with guilt, I dove into the kitchen to collect an order that was up for another of my tables. I returned to find that in my absence the couple had taken more bottles down, and now held one in each hand, shaking them like maracas. I hurried over.

"Can I, uh, get you anything else?" I asked.

"Take a look," the man said, offering one of his bottles. His girlfriend made small fascinated noises as she continued to rattle hers. Were they stoned? What they were, it turns out, was revolted. I could see why. At the bottom of the bottle, six legs pointing stiffly toward the ceiling, was a dead cockroach. People at the surrounding tables, their curiosity piqued, were reaching for the bottles nearest them. A quick visual check revealed that every bottle on the ledge boasted at least one cancelled *cucaracha.*

I darted into the kitchen to alert the boss. "Dave! Dave! We've got a problem! Everybody in my section is shaking the bottles! They're all full of roaches, dead roaches!"

"Oh, gnarly!" Tommy the cook cried happily. "It must've been the exterminator! He was here yesterday fogging for bugs. That's so fucking gross!"

Dave sighed and wiped his hands on his T-shirt before stretching another lump of pizza dough to fit the pan. "Well, buddy, what do you suggest I do about it?"

"I don't know! Can I offer them a free chocolate mousse or something?"

"Sure, buddy, if that's what you want," Dave mumbled, no doubt realizing that for every mousse I comped a customer, I'd help myself to two.

I miss Dave's more than any of the other places I worked. I miss the money and finding crumpled twenties in my pockets every time I did the laundry. I miss the checkered tablecloths and the bottles, which were recycled the morning after the roaches were discovered. I miss the phone numbers scrawled on the kitchen walls and waiting on other waiters who'd come in after their shifts at Hecky's and the Blind Faith Café. I don't miss the Piggies, nor do I miss the sauce-cheeked toddlers who threw grubby handfuls of cut-up spaghetti onto the brown industrial carpeting beneath booth 11. Now *I'm* the criminal who takes young children into restaurants, hoping my broad smile telegraphs the juicy tip I will bestow to counteract the annoyance I've visited on the establishment. I rarely go a day without revisiting that sensation of being in the weeds. Judy and Gert used to look down their blow-worn noses at me because I could balance only three plates on my arm, but in the domestic setting, this is an impressive feat. Imperiling my own china in the name of vanity, I tell my dinner guests that old waitresses never die. Waiting tables was kind of like doing low-budget theater—physically grueling, often humiliating, but then when you haven't done it in a while, you remember all the good times you had at the bar afterward. Most of all, I miss the sense of absolute freedom that came when I boarded the El at one in the morning, reeking of sweat and creamy garlic dressing, rehashing everything my fellow waiter, Isaac, had said to me, the way his shoulders moved beneath his shirt when he sliced bread. I had a wad of cash in my bra and a large free-of-charge pizza in the box on my lap.

One night, a drunk homeless guy teasingly asked me for a slice. To his surprise, I lifted the lid and invited all our fellow passengers to help themselves. I have never felt more professionally powerful than I did at that moment—even though the homeless guy wrinkled his nose when he saw the anchovies.

lonely little petunia in an onion patch

Selling hippie clothing seemed like a great way to meet people. And it probably would have been if I'd been selling it out of a van in the parking lot of a Grateful Dead show. I didn't lack for friends, but they tended to be tart-tongued wisenheimers with high reference levels, hardly the sort to burn sandalwood while listening to Joni Mitchell and boiling up a vat of dye. I looked to Moondancer to provide some necessary balance in my social life, but unfortunately, there were rarely any customers in the store to prevent me from trying on the latest shipment of patchouli-scented gauze. I offered to design an ad to run in the local alternative weekly, but the owner, a wealthy suburbanite who made frequent references to goddesses and angels, showed little interest in attracting more business. Perhaps it's not the place of a lowly wage slave to speculate, but Moondancer stank of tax shelter from the second it hung out its shingle, or rather, its rainbow. The rainbow was a spectral projection that had been purchased at great expense from some outfit in Santa Fe. By day it was invisible, but it showed up on the sidewalk after dark, a lonely little petunia in an onion patch whose nocturnal denizens had little truck with the New Age. One whole side of Glenwood was taken up by the El tracks. The streetlamps opposite were too busy submitting to vandals and promoting lousy bands to provide much in the way of illumination. The rainbow was pissed on, barfed on, bled on, and ignored, while neighboring businesses did a brisk trade in crack pipes and Mad Dog 20/20. Rather than reaching out to that decidedly non-Aquarian community, I opted to lie on the floor behind the wooden display cases, sloppily picnicking on takeout from Morse Chop Suey.

Maybe Vicki hoped her store could survive parasitically on the Heartland Café, a legendary eatery on the next block whose rooftop whirligigs and Christmas lights were visible from the Morse El platform. The Heartland had been in business so long that its original young customers now drove Beemers in from the northern suburbs, accompanied by disdainful adolescent children whose love might need to be purchased with a pair of dangly earrings just like the ones Mommy wore in 1972. Unfortunately for Vicki, the Heartland, in addition to hosting bands and art shows, also maintained a well-stocked general store, enabling diners to take care of their Guatemalan apparel needs along with the bill for their vegetarian chili. The Heartland sold books, videos, and bulk coffee, too, all of it benefiting the Sandinistas in some way. Why venture down Glenwood to Moondancer, where one was sure to find the lone clerk sprawled on the floor, her dirty bare feet propped on the counter, as she gorged on shrimp fried rice from a Styrofoam container? We sold the same shit they did, for more.

It had been my dream to get a job at the Heartland, but I made the mistake of telling the manager that I was an actor. "Uh-uh," he scowled, "sorry," as he tore my application to bits right in front of me. "I'm sure you're a very nice person and all, but come on! I put time and effort into training you only to find out that *pffft,* you've gotten yourself a role in some play? Suddenly it's, 'Oh, I'm afraid I can't work nights for the next three weeks because I've got rehearsal . . . .' No way. I've got enough shit to deal with around here without taking on another thespian."

Once the cat was out of the bag, there was no convincing the managerial hard-ass that I wasn't much of an actor. Oh sure, I went on auditions that I read about in the Classifieds section of the free alternative weekly available in the Heartland's foyer, but my chances of getting cast were slim to none! No dice. Tough guy wasn't interested in hearing the odds.

When I applied to work at Moondancer, however, I met with an entirely different reaction. Vicki considered actors to be "people people" and thus better suited to retail than just plain people. My training went well in her flagship store, a slightly less fairy-encrusted enterprise in the leafy suburb she called home. "It's like you've got a sixth sense. I just knew you'd be a natural," she congratulated us both after I talked a tennis-skirted mother into adding one more beaded scarf to her college-bound daughter's pile. I modestly squirted some glass cleaner on a clean cotton diaper to wipe an afternoon's worth of nose prints off the jewelry case. "You're a treasure," Vicki marveled, with the confidence of someone quite used to finding treasures and paying them $5.25 an hour.

After three days, I was transferred back to the Glenwood Avenue Moondancer and left to my own devices. I saw Vicki once a week, when she dropped off merchandise and picked up the envelopes of cash and credit card transactions I'd been instructed to store in the back pocket of a three-ring binder. With no supervision, I instantly reverted. I know some salespeople follow in their customers' wake, tidying up, but I didn't want to risk scaring off the few walk-ins we got by breathing down their necks. Besides, if I'd had that big of a hard-on for refolding sweaters, I'd have gotten a job at the Gap (assuming they'd hire someone who hadn't shaved her legs since high school). Like me, Moondancer's stock looked best crumpled in a heap on the floor. I specialized in window displays that looked like Bedouin yard sales. Until familiarity bred contempt, doing the windows was my favorite part of the job, the realization of a professional fantasy I'd harbored in third grade. Unlike Mary Tyler Moore's best friend, Rhoda Morgenstern, I didn't get to contend with any haughty mannequins. Anything that didn't spill out of willow baskets dangled limply on hangers suspended from the hemp ropes Vicki's husband, Herb, had nailed to the tin ceiling. "The window looks so messy," Vicki wailed on one of her weekly visits. Was she forgetting that I was a treasure? Herb, double-parked in the Wagoneer, honked impatiently. "Ayun, can't you give it some more, I don't know, *flair?*"

Who did she think I was, Holly Golightly? We were peddling tie-dyed fanny packs and twenty-dollar T-shirts embroidered by Nepali children to a clientele whose daily numbers rarely exceeded the low single digits. *Flair* seemed better suited to a different species of retail, the kind that took out full-page ads in the *Tribune* to herald the approach of Easter. Clearly, Vicki's heart was not with the rebellion. Still, I humored her by fussing with the display until the Wagoneer turned the corner, and then I returned to the stack of underground comics I had stashed beneath a pile of Peruvian sweaters when the clatter of wind chimes had alerted me to her arrival.

Once I'd realized that Moondancer wasn't going to catapult me to the center of a Heartland-style hippie social scene, I was more than happy to spend the days reading. Given the choice of Windex or *Love in the Time of Cholera*, I inevitably reached for chopsticks first, book second. Windex, not at all.

It is a sad reality that readers tend to attract chatty nonreaders, much in the same way that solitary clerks in dead hippie-clothing stores are sitting ducks for neighborhood philosophers, conspiracy theorists, and assorted other cranks. People who couldn't afford the price of the drink to monopolize a bartender's ear recognized a free captive audience in me. I'd say one out of every four old men with mosslike tufts sprouting from his ears and nostrils who came through the door blundered in by mistake. The others marched in purposefully to lecture me on the rise of fascism or the intellectual bankruptcy of the abstract expressionists. Even though I'd been raised to be polite, I couldn't help slumping across the jewelry counter, my face a mask of impertinent boredom, lest something in my manner encourage repeat visits. The *charming* elderly eccentrics who are such a staple of Hollywood films must have lived in another neighborhood, or else they were shut-ins—if they existed at all. The moth-eaten fellows who bent my ear were pitiable for being desperately lonely, but they were also misanthropic, self-righteous, and determined not to yield the floor to anyone, least of all some long-haired girlie in a shapeless dress that looked like something from the Old World. I felt I had more than an inkling about why they had wound up alone in studio apartments stuffed with towering stacks of yellowing newspapers. *Please go away,* I pleaded silently. *Leave me alone. Go bother Chet.*

Chet, though half a century younger, was exactly like them, full of off-putting pride, obscure factoids, and the uncontrollable desire to soliloquize. I knew this because Chet was also a frequent visitor. The used-bookstore-cum-tea-parlor he'd opened on the other side of Morse Chop Suey was faring even worse than Moondancer. He'd managed to make a dismal location even worse with a saggy, flesh-colored couch he'd dragged to the center of his selling floor, a close cousin of those stained stuffed animals one goes out of one's way not to touch in thrift stores. The lounging bibliophiles he sought to accommodate with this monstrous sofa failed to materialize, perhaps because his book selection was even more paltry than the variety of teas he had on offer—just a couple of shelves devoted to the occult, with nary an original dust jacket on display. I kept waiting for Chet to lay in more stock, but instead he devoted an entire week to painting the metal accordion grate over his front window an uninviting shade of baby blue. Then he made a beeline for Moondancer to tell me all about it. "You should paint your grate," he snorted contemptuously, making himself comfy on a low table stacked with Baja hoodies.

"Careful, man. Watch the clothes," I said wearily.

Heaving a put-upon sigh, he relocated to the counter, enveloping me in a cloud of overpowering stink. It's sad that my olfactory memories of Moondancer are tainted with the essence of Chet. Otherwise, from a nasal standpoint, it was a dream job for someone like me. Am I the only one who thinks that flimsy Indian cotton smells great? You know, that exotic sandalwood musk that no amount of Western detergent can obliterate? It's a total Proustian rush for me, every whiff returning me to the summer between junior and senior years of high school, when I bought a pair of purple harem pants flecked with gold paint from a man in a turban who gave me a discount for paying in cash. When I later traveled to India, I was thrilled to find that Indian cotton smells exactly the same over there. It's a powerful aroma—but so was Chet's. Simply put, he smelled like a never-ending fart on a crowded public bus. It might have been a defense mechanism. Aren't there toads that secrete a poisonous reek to make sure they're left alone?

Why did Chet come bother me all the time when he had a business of his own to run? "Isn't it obvious?" Isaac asked, raising an eyebrow. "He's got a crush on you."

He smiled with quiet satisfaction as my flesh crawled out the door and down the block, coming to a stop midway between Chet's baby-blue grate and the Heartland. "He wants to take off all his clothes and lick you all over."

"Oh god, he does not."

"Yes, he wants you to put your nose in the crinkly red hairs of his sweaty crack."

"Shut up."

"He wants to squat over you and—"

"Isaac, quit it! He does not."

"Oh, he wants to," Isaac insisted, sidling over to where I stood closing out the register. He nuzzled my neck with his long pony nose, then ground his pelvis against my rump in a manner most uncharacteristic. "Oh, unh-huh. Oh, yeah. That's right. Unh-huh. You like it hobbit-style?"

"Cut it out! You're going to make me lose my count!"

"Yeah, there must be at least fifty dollars in that drawer."

"Excuse me, I have two credit card receipts to add up. We can't leave until I've entered them into the report."

"You don't really think Chet likes me in that way, do you?" I asked later that night, as we lay several inches above the floor on the king-sized mattress that dominated my studio apartment, conveniently located less than half a block away from Moondancer.

Isaac propped himself up on a skinny elbow. "I think he's

got good instincts. He can tell you're much nicer than those mean cheerleader types who have made his life a misery."

"I'm mean to him."

"Do you tell him that his body looks like a yam?"

"I don't even pretend to like him."

"Do you call him Bilbo? Do you ask if he's a dwarf?"

"I wouldn't mind him hanging around all the time if he didn't act so superior. He's like this kid who got skipped a grade to my class when I was in elementary school. Arnie Fink. He was the smartest kid in the class, but he had to be a total asshole about it, never letting you forget how superior he was. God, I can still see his smirking, pudgy face."

"Pudgy, huh?" Isaac squeezed one of my generous haunches lasciviously. "Ooh, just like Chet. You know you want him."

"Why are you acting this way? I don't 'want' Chet."

"Yes. You like his smell. You want to stick your nose into all of his sweaty Chet crevices," he insisted gleefully as I sprang shrieking to the farthest corner of the apartment.

The next day, the bell over the door tinkled as I was in the dressing room trying on the latest batch of sundresses from a company called Bali Dolly. Isaac and I were trying to save up enough money to get to Southeast Asia, and Bali Dolly had me all jacked up to go to Indonesia. I pictured it as a tropical paradise where women floated around in black rayon shifts printed with ankhs and yin yangs. "Make yourself at home," I called to the unseen customer, as I struggled with a cheap zipper. "I'll be out in a sec." A familiar scent wafted through the dressing-room curtains. Shit. Chet.

I shuffled out, rubbing my temples, hoping that I could get him to leave by feigning a migraine. He wasn't alone. A tall kid with a ponytail and Dickensian mutton chops was trying out a hardwood kaleidoscope from the Amazonian rain forest. "Whoa, this thing is seriously trippy," he announced. "Chet, look over here!" Rolling his eyes for my benefit, Chet turned toward his friend with an indulgent sneer. "Oh no!" the boy yelped happily. "Wow! I just wish you could see what I'm seeing, bro. It's like a hundred little Chet heads all spinning around on their little axises."

Chet grimaced up at the ceiling, a fog of sewer gas seeping past his tea-stained teeth. "I should never have agreed to go into a business partnership," he mused. Then, to his friend: "This is that girl I was telling you about."

Chet's friend lowered the kaleidoscope. "My lady," he said, extending his hand so that he could press mine to his lips. "Name's Wizard."

"What?" Thanks to Isaac, I was paralyzed. What exactly had Chet been telling him about me, that I was totally hot for him, that he'd had his gnome-like way with me on that earwig-infested couch?

"Wizard, like the store," he grinned. I stared at him blankly. "Mystical Wizard's Tomes and Teas?" A bit of the mean cheerleader crept into his disbelieving tone, sort of like the popular girls ganging up on Carrie because she doesn't know what her period is.

"Oh, right, the bookstore. Sorry, I blanked out on the name," I apologized, returning the kaleidoscope to its velvet-lined case.

"Chet was saying you're thinking about painting your grate like ours."

"No-o-o."

Chet seized the kaleidoscope, training it angrily on Wizard, then on me. The tips of his freckled ears flushed scarlet. "I hate to tell you, but I don't think you're going to find anyone stupid enough to pay seventy-five dollars for this thing," he announced, with the zeal of someone desperate to change the subject.

"Chet, I don't *care* if anyone buys it." I snatched the Windex from the shelf beneath the register in an attempt to send a passive-aggressive message about him and his grubby paws. "I just work here."

"You shouldn't be afraid to open your own business," the clueless Wizard enthused. "I'm here to tell you, it's not as hard as you think. Look at us! He's twenty-two. I'm nineteen. You know, like Mr. Society's out there telling us, 'You! Put on a paper hat and make me a Big Mac', but we're like, 'Excuse me, I don't think so.' No Burger King for us, not with our skills. Like, Chet knows so much more about Wicca and the druids and Aleister Crowley than most forty-year-olds, it's not even funny, okay?"

"Okay." I gathered my lunch debris to take to the back, where a lidded garbage can had been positioned to thwart the neighborhood rats, or "mice," as Vicki preferred to call them. When I wasn't trying to get rid of pesky visitors, I tended to be pretty cavalier about disposing of my leftovers. What rat would take the trouble of squeezing through our back transom, considering the giant unsanitary spread going on next door at Morse Chop Suey?

"What are you doing? You can't follow me in here."

"Oops, sorry." Wizard retreated to the doorway, holding the celestial-pattern drapes open so we could continue our conversation.

"Why can't he go back there?" Chet challenged, crowding in beside his friend. "Are you running some sort of top-secret experiment on alien beings that the FBI doesn't want us to know about?"

Now my inner mean cheerleader was rising to the surface.

"Chet, in case you haven't noticed, this is a business. Certain areas are off-limits to people who don't work here. If my boss were to drive up right now, I would get in trouble because of your apparently burning desire to see where we store the vacuum cleaner."

"Ooh, *trouble,*" Chet snickered. Wizard guffawed appreciatively, chiming in in a higher, more feminine register. "Ooh, trouble, I'm so scared!"

I shoved past them, returning to stand sentry over the kaleidoscope. "If I were you, I'd be back at my store, getting my pentacles sorted and brewing up a big pot of newt eyeballs. Wouldn't want the big rush to catch me unawares."

"Yes, well, that's why we went into business for ourselves," Chet explained, speaking slowly as if reminding an illiterate high school English class why Shakespeare is important. "*We* don't *have* a boss telling us *when* we can take breaks or *who* we can let into our back room. It's a completely autonomous model. The only person we have to answer to is each other. If one of us—"

"Right," Wizard interrupted. "He does books. I do tea. That's my thing. If you ever want to know anything about any kind of tea—and I'm talking any tea in the world, Darjeeling, oolong, herbal, green—you just ask me, because that's, like, my passion. Like, if you were wondering why you haven't seen me before, it's because I spent the last three weeks traveling around getting all the different teas for the store. I don't mean tea bags, okay?" He whinnied, thrashing his ponytail. "*Bags,* right! 'Can I have a tea bag? Can I have some Lipton's?' I'd be like, 'I'm sorry. No. Leave.'"

"So, where did you go to get it?" I asked resignedly.

"Michigan."

"Michigan."

"Yeah, my dad lives there with his new wife."

"You didn't go anywhere else?"

"I was going to go down to Springfield. This dude I know works in an herb store, and he said he could fix me up with several big-ass bales of chamomile. But my dad's car broke down, so it'll have to wait."

"Bummer."

We all jumped as someone rapped hard on the plate-glass window. It was Isaac, on his way to the El station, wearing the wrinkled button-down shirt he wore to wait tables at Dave's. He cocked his head almost imperceptibly at Chet, raising his eyebrow suggestively and blowing a kiss. He skipped away before I could make it out to the sidewalk.

"Do you know that guy?"

"Yeah, he's my boyfriend."

Wizard pretended to stab himself in the heart. "Why are the beautiful ones always taken?" he howled as he sank to his knees.

"Get up," Chet hissed, nudging his fallen partner with his stubby sneakers. "If Mitchell stops by with that bookcase and we're not there, he might change his mind about letting you use his car." He banged out the door without saying goodbye.

Wizard scrambled to his feet. "Come by later and I'll prepare you a perfect pot of chai. That's Indian for 'tea'!" he called over his shoulder as I applied the hem of a paisley wraparound skirt to the lower half of my face like a surgical mask, a little ritual I'd worked up to purify the nasal membranes following an encounter with Chet.

A couple of weeks later, Vicki surprised me by giving me a friend. Her name was Willa, and she had been hired in anticipation of the upcoming Christmas season. Maybe Moondancer's suburban flagship was mobbed with holiday shoppers, but the Glenwood outpost afforded its new employee scant opportunities for actual hands-on experience. "What do you do all day if nobody comes in?" Willa frowned, having refolded every sweater and scarf on the rough wooden shelves.

"I read. I get takeout from next door. Sometimes my boyfriend comes to hang out. I used to try stuff on, but I can barely stand to look at it anymore."

"It's so materialistic," Willa agreed, the picture of socialist virtue in granny glasses and non-leather clogs.

"You're welcome to try things on if you see anything you like."

"Really?" She immediately yanked a voluminous poet's shirt out of the window. On me, it added forty matronly pounds, but I could tell it would look nice on Willa's militantly vegetarian frame.

"Sure. Give me a fashion show. Take it home with you if you want." She scampered, giggling, into the dressing room, weighted down like a gypsy caravan's washerwoman.

We had a lot of fun, me and Willa, even though she failed to see how I could call myself a feminist when I yukked it up over the likes of R. Crumb and Peter Bagge. Fortunately, a deep vein of corruption snaked through her alabaster convictions, leavening her solidarity with various oppressed indigenous peoples and her adoration of an environmentally conscious but talent-free free-form vegan band. She could lie on the floor eating egg rolls and doing crosswords like a pro. She boosted Scotch tape and toilet paper. Whereas I joked about bringing in a thermos of cocktails with no real plans to do so, Willa had no qualms about dipping into her Tibetan stash bag on Moondancer's nickel. Her habit of curling up in the front window to separate stems from seeds was unnerving, but also foolproof. Lawmen were a rarity on Glenwood, and little Willa was innocence incarnate, perched there in her purloined yak-hair pullover, the afternoon sun coaxing golden highlights from the thick bangs obscuring her spectacles. Loading her pinch hitter, she looked as wholesome as a schoolgirl finishing her math homework before the start of her candy-striper shift.

The most shocking thing about Willa was her ability to fend off Chet. Shortly after she started working at Moondancer, she banged through the door, looking even more disgusted than she did when discussing the Contras or the Republican National Committee. "You'll never guess who I just bumped into," she said.

"Abbie Hoffman?" I asked hopefully. Willa had recently broken it off with a son of the Chicago Seven, the lead singer for Eco Jam, the vegan band.

"No, you know that weird used bookstore that barely has any books in it?" I nodded. "Okay, well, when I was at Oberlin, there was this awful little troll—literally—who used to crash our parties and then stand around berating us."

"Chet. I'm well acquainted with him. He comes in here all the time."

"He does? That makes me want to vomit. Does he still smell?" I nodded again. "That's revolting. I can't believe you let him in here."

"Am I hearing you correctly? Are you saying that Moondancer should practice discrimination?" I chucked a headband trimmed with Guatemalan worry dolls at her.

"That's exactly what I'm saying," she confirmed, putting the headband on. She picked up the antique hand mirror from the counter and examined her reflection. "What kind of dork wears something like this?"

Willa remained true to her word. When Chet came in later that day, she refused to join in his admittedly less-than-gracious expression of wonder that two recent grads of Oberlin should find themselves working on the same Chicago street. "You're not still in touch with that guy who was in that stupid Save the Whales band, are you?" he inquired.

"Was there something in particular you were looking for?" Willa countered.

"Uh, no," Chet sneered. "I can't say as I get the appeal of the whole hippie thing. That's more of your musician friend's—"

"Then get out." Amazingly, he did, shooting me a reproachful look on the way.

"Damn, Willa, that was cold," I observed admiringly. At college I'd seen young activists prone to denouncing absent imperialist policymakers at peace project meetings politely shaking hands with some of these same policymakers' top dogs on Parents Weekend. I didn't blame them for allowing their passionate convictions to crumble in the face of social imperative. I'd been raised to do the same. I'd never have expected Willa to be capable of expressing such withering derision in a one-on-one situation, but sometimes mean cheerleaders turn up in the unlikeliest of forms. Maybe she could give me lessons.

"Get the Lysol," she commanded. "That stench has to be eradicated immediately or we'll never get rid of it."

Willa also excelled at bagging shoplifters and repelling the wild-eyed entrepreneurs who barged in off the street, intent on selling us all sorts of hot but unexciting goods, everything from coloring books to corn pads, often with the price stickers from the ancient pharmacy on the corner still attached. I was far more laissez-faire. I refunded a cute, stoned Deadhead in full for a pair of badly ripped, mud-caked, patchouli-saturated tie-dyed trousers. Far be it from me to accuse him of lying, even if he claimed they split as he lifted his knee to knock his Hacky Sack just five short minutes into the pants' first wearing. I let a homeless woman change her sanitary napkin in the dressing room. I gave a poor soul named Cosmic Twinkie hope that Vicki might place an order for the ugly beaded necklaces she strung on plastic lanyards. My charitable lack of backbone made Willa insane.

By this time Christmas was over, and Willa and I had been put on separate details, though frequently the one who wasn't working that day would show up to spell the other for an hour or two, however long was required to do a load of laundry or meet friends for a leisurely lunch at the Heartland. Once, when Willa was alone at the helm, a none-too-tidy fellow wandered in and announced, "I'm Jesus Christ and I'm here to fuck you." Somehow she managed to hustle the self-proclaimed Messiah's two-hundred-plus pounds back onto the street before he could implement his plan, but she called Vicki to demand that a security buzzer be installed on the door so that we lone workers could protect ourselves from the Son of God and other unsavory characters. Request denied. Vicki was still pissed about the time she had swung by to drop off some sequined Thai coin purses, only to discover us sprawled behind the counter amid noodle refuse, wearing elaborate crowns we'd spent all afternoon fashioning from pipe cleaners. (That was the incident that had prompted the separate shifts.) "She claimed it would be way too expensive to get a buzzer," Willa reported, outraged.

"Just wait until you sue her after Jesus Christ murders you in the dressing room," I said consolingly. "Then she'll know the meaning of 'expensive'."

"Yeah, well, she won't get the chance. I gave her my notice."

"No! You can't quit! What about me?"

"You should quit, too." Willa struck a defiant pose. I looked around. Somehow, I couldn't imagine spending my days anywhere else. Who else would pay me to lie around eating, surrounded by such agreeably boho dry goods? My lack of resolve got Willa's dander up. "Ayun, do you really want to work for a boss who cares so little for the welfare of her workers?"

"Willa, short of Ben and Jerry, nobody cares about their workers. Please don't quit. I'll call Vicki and tell her to put in a security system."

Willa gestured to the phone. I dialed the suburban mother ship. "Vicki, hi, it's Ayun. Listen, I think you should really reconsider getting us some sort of buzzer or something on the door—"

Willa smirked when I hung up. "Well?"

"She said her decision was final. She accused me of wanting to keep customers out so I could lie around eating."

"You don't need a buzzer for that," declared Willa, whom Vicki now made a point of referring to as my 'little friend'.

A few days later, Willa called me at Isaac's. "Can you meet me at Moondancer?" she asked. "Somebody broke in last night." I pulled on my clothes and raced over, arriving just as a squad car pulled up on Glenwood. The jewelry cases had been smashed and picked clean. Even the velvet ring trays were gone. The boom box was gone. The cash register drawer gaped open. "Look, they took all those pressed-velvet shawls that came in last week," Willa murmured, pointing to an empty shelf. "I was thinking about absconding with one of those myself."

"Yeah, well, don't tell them that," I said, rolling my eyes toward the burly young policemen clumping around in their polished black boots. "Oh shit, look who's here."

"Oh, no. Out," Willa commanded, as Chet picked his way around the broken glass, lugging a milk crate full of musty-smelling books. "I mean it, Chet."

"Officer, I'm a neighboring business owner," Chet announced, turning his back on Willa, who gaped at me in disbelief, then covered her nostrils with the cowl of her oversized sweater. The cop rolled back on his heels, an amused expression on his handsome, meaty face. "If there's been a robbery, I have a right to be informed."

"Go *home,* Chet," Willa threatened, through a thick layer of cable-knit wool.

"Yeah, somebody came in through that little transom window over the alley door," the cop said. "Just propped a ladder against the wall and dropped into the back room. You should really get that transom nailed shut, Miss."

"I'm not the owner," Willa told him.

He looked at me. I shook my head. "That's the owner," I said, as Herb's Wagoneer pulled up outside, spilling out a hyperventilating Vicki.

"Look what those animals did," she wept, caressing the wooden stand that had held the kaleidoscope. "I feel like I've been raped! Oh, all my beautiful earrings!" Out of the corner of my eye, I noticed Willa discreetly slipping the teardrop-shaped bloodstones from her lobes and dropping them in her pocket. I felt my own holes for any incriminating evidence, but fortunately my earrings had been left on the side of Isaac's sink. "Oh my god, it's exactly like I've been raped," Vicki repeated. "Do you have any idea how this feels?"

"I'm sure your insurance will cover it," I consoled Vicki.

"That's not the point," she snapped tearfully. "Somebody violated my private space! It's like I was *raped!*"

The cops exchanged weary glances. They were used to dealing with homeless Vietnam vets who'd gone off their meds and domestically abused crackheads, but this pampered suburban matron was turning into a real handful. I was interested to see how Vicki would react when it dawned on her that her precious guardian angel had let her down. Maybe the angel had raped her, too.

"Well, if you don't need me for anything else, I guess I'll head back home," Willa ventured.

"Oh my god, my rainbow," Vicki yelped. I looked at the ceiling. The stamped-tin panels where the projection box had been suspended were oddly torqued.

"Must have used a crowbar to pry it loose," the policemen speculated after Willa and I explained what was missing, since Vicki was incoherent with grief. "What should I call it?" the taller one asked his partner, pausing over the form on which he was itemizing Moondancer's losses. "Would you describe it as looking like a slide projector?" He waited, his Bic poised in expectation.

"It wasn't a slide projector," Vicki snarled. "It was a *rainbow generator!* It had three prisms!"

Even Chet snorted. To my amazement, Willa smiled. "Okay, I'm going," she announced, slipping out the door before Vicki could object. It took me half a second to remember that I was under no obligation to stay. I wasn't getting paid for my time. "Willa, wait up," I called, banging after her, a cacophony of miniature Peruvian wind chimes flagellating themselves in my wake.

gilberto rides an elephant

“Es-cuse me,” the woman seated next to me called to the proctor while the test booklets were still being passed out among the back rows. “What do we put where it say ‘County’?”

My fellow examinees and I were sitting in a room filled with molded plastic chairs, the kind with attached desktops. I’d psyched myself up for this aspect of the lengthy application process. A fellow graduate of Northwestern’s theater department who supported himself as a substitute teacher had given me the lowdown, warning me about the many irritating bureaucratic hoops through which I’d be expected to jump—everything from being fingerprinted to taking a tuberculosis test. “Don’t worry,” he’d scoffed when I fretted about passing the exam the Board of Ed administered to all would-be subs. "You could pass that thing with your eyes closed." He gnawed thoughtfully on his lower lip. "You don't have TB, do you?"

"Do not start filling out your test booklet until I *tell* you to," the proctor boomed, addressing the entire group. "Once everyone has received their booklet, I will give the order to pick up your pencils, and then we will fill out the first page together." Several hands shot up. The proctor shook his head in disdain. "If you still have questions after we have filled the first page out, *together*, then you can raise your hands. After everyone has finished the first page, you will have two hours to complete the exam. If you have to go to the bathroom, go now, because you will not be allowed to go during the exam. Now, does everyone see a blank that says 'Last Name'? Go ahead and fill your last name in there." More hands shot up.

I slumped in my posture-deforming chair, thinking about my second-grade teacher, Mrs. Morse, who had us role-play that we were ancient Mesopotamians and rewarded exceptional extracurricular reading with orange gumdrops. I was reminded too of the training session I had attended as a newly hired T.J. Maxx cashier in a banquet room at the Evanston Holiday Inn. I went for two of the three scheduled days before coming to my senses. Those two days had also involved synchronized form-filling-out, in between film strips on such ethically complex topics as "Employee Theft: Right or Wrong?"

At last, the group arrived at the blank that had hamstrung the aspirant educator to my left. "That's Cook, C-O-O-K, County," the proctor said, enunciating fiercely as if daring one of us to fuck this up. "Don't put 'County.' Just put 'Cook.' Cook County."

"Oh, like the hospital," someone exclaimed, as a lightbulb went on in the row behind me.

Or the prison, I thought.

job hopper

The call came at the crack of dawn, rousing me after just a few hours of sleep. A bilingual classroom on the far West Side, mixed level, first and second graders. Could I be there by 7:45 for an 8:00 bell? "Uh . . . yeah," I muttered, searching for a pen to take down the address. Only after I hung up did it occur to me, *Zut alors! Ils ne sont probablement pas* bilingual *en français, n'est-ce pas?*

When I arrived, the kids were running around in circles, screaming. No problem—my friend had told me to expect this. Ten minutes later, they were still running around screaming. All except for two dark-eyed little girls who sat politely at their desks, waiting for me to bring their fellows to heel. I tried. "Good morning!" I shouted as I printed my name across the chalkboard. "My name is Ms. Halliday! But it's okay if you want to call me Ayun! And, uh, *no hablo español,* so please sit down so we can begin! I know you're having fun, but as soon as you're all in your chairs, we can start to have *more* fun!" Hoo, boy, tough crowd. "Let's all sit down now, okay?" I begged. *"Asseyez! Asseyez-vous!"* Shit, I guess the Romance languages weren't as closely related as Madame Karnowsky had led us to believe back in high school. "Time to sit down now, boys and girls!" I repeated, reverting to my native language and clapping my hands. Nobody showed the slightest signs of slowing down, but I knew they'd taken notice, because rising above the general hubbub of girlish squeals and piping obscenities, I could detect delighted cries. "A sub! A sub!" I shrank against the board as a pair of particularly wild boys streaked past, limbs flailing. The one with the Caesar haircut stretched out his arm, hooked the waistband of the kid he'd been chasing, and they both crashed to the ground, rolling into the front row of desks. "Fuck you,

you stupid *pendejo,*" the quarry yelled, furious tears springing to his eyes as he and Caesar grappled.

"Okay, that's enough!" I barked, hauling Caesar off the other kid by his armpits. "Everybody get in your seats NOW! I MEAN it! Or I'll tell your teacher!" This outburst was apparently sufficiently impressive to send half of them tumbling toward their seats, laughing and chattering. Jesus. The manual the Board of Ed had supplied in advance of this first posting spelled out exactly what to do if a student arrived late (don't admit him without a signed late slip) or pulled a knife (take your purse and leave) but didn't offer a single tip for marshaling thirty-five unruly six- and seven-year-olds. "You!" Caesar was still squirming in my arms, his small face delirious with pleasure. "What's your name?" He seemed to be pushing toward trilingualism with some sort of gibberish, perhaps a dialectical variation of nanny-nanny-boo-boo. "What is your name?" I demanded again.

"That's Gilberto," one of the first-to-be-seated little girls spoke up. "He's a bad boy."

"Where does he sit?" I asked. She pointed solemnly to a spot in the back row as Gilberto, catcalling to several of his comrades, strained to break free. "Thank you." I frog-marched him to his assigned seat and pressed him into it, mindful of the edict against anything that might be construed as corporeal punishment. "Gilberto, sit," I hissed. "Stay." He bolted, but I'd anticipated this and managed to snag him by the elbow. "Sit. Down." Fuck, man. Still gripping his scrawny shoulders, I took stock of the situation. With the exception of the natural submissives, Teresa and Blanca, they were all back out of their seats, running around in circles. Shouting.

According to the schedule I'd been given, I was to take attendance between 8:05 and 8:15. I managed to complete it at around 10:00, and then only because Teresa had taken it upon herself to inform me when someone was out sick or pulling my leg or so freaked out to be in a new apartment and a new country that they were incapable of uttering so much as a simple "here." Snapping the roll book shut, I opened the lesson plan. We were slated to build simple sentences together, but the clunkers the teacher's guide wanted me to use left me cold. "Jim throws a ball. Sally sweeps the floor." Not only did they reinforce tired gender stereotypes, they were about as exciting as linoleum. I pictured Chris, my mentor in all things sub related, leaping around with his pint-sized inmates. He was funny and creative and bore more than a passing resemblance to Wallace Shawn. I bet old Chris hadn't stuck to the script when constructing simple sentences. I couldn't imagine Jim and Sally piquing anyone's interest anymore, least of all children whose taste of the white-bread experience had been scanty at best. "Okay, boys and girls," I blared, feeling reinvigorated by the chance to redeem myself. "We're going to continue the sentence work you've been doing, but we're going to have some fun with it! Who wants to be in a sentence?" No hands went up, but by this stage of the game, my low-budget-improv-based theater skills were such that I not only knew, but accepted, the score on audience participation. Most people are too chicken to volunteer—it's almost always the performer's responsibility to select a victim. "Gilberto! Come on up here," I commanded jovially. If nothing else, the kid had proven himself to be uninhibited. Maybe he'd simmer down if I appealed to his ego, showed him that there were positive ways to be the center of attention. It took a while to separate him from the chum he'd been sparring with when we met, but eventually I managed to drag him with me up to the board. I kept a firm grip on his wrist as I chalked his name under mine. "Okay! Gilberto's going to be the subject of our sentence!" Were these guys too little to know about subjects and predicates and verbs and such, especially when English wasn't their first language? I couldn't remember if we'd gotten into that with Mrs. Morse, though I vividly recalled learning the metric system with something called "cuillere" rods and a story in the *Scholastic Weekly Reader* about these mud-filled mattresses that had been specially designed for burn victims. "All right, Gilberto, tell us what you like to do." He ignored me to chatter at some of his cronies in fluent but incomprehensible nanny-nanny-boo-boo. "If you could do anything in the world right now, Gilberto . . ." I prompted hopefully, fishing for the rest of the sentence. "Do you like . . . to eat spaghetti?" Nada. Dang, when I was a kid, adults always seemed to get a laugh with spaghetti. Maybe these guys didn't eat spaghetti. No doubt they regularly ingested something just as hilarious, but I didn't presume to know what that cultural equivalent might be. Instead, I pressed on to the gross. Little boys get a bang out of disgusting things, right? Instinctively certain that I'd regret it if I introduced bodily fluids, I groped around for something more innocuous but still suitably slimy and unappetizing. "How about . . . do you like to . . . dig for worms so you can go fishing with Grandpa?" I wiggled my fingers in a manner most bait like. No reaction, not even from the girliest girls. "Worms!" Hey, hey, you've been a wonderful audience! Thank you and good night! It's rare that I find myself craving alcoholic refreshment in advance of lunch.

"He like to watch TV," a dough-faced boy who looked to be at least fourteen called from the back. Several others nodded enthusiastically.

"Okay, thanks," I hedged. "But I think what we're looking for here is something a little more active. Anybody want to help us out here? No? Okay, *I* know what Gilberto likes to do!" Shuffling through a host of possibilities, I paused for dramatic effect, accidentally relaxing my hold on Gilberto, who sped off yowling, as self-destructive as Squirrel Nutkin. "Gilberto," I continued doggedly, "likes to ride . . . an elephant!" I beamed at the few who were still paying attention. Hey! Hey, kids, is that a knee-slapper or what! I braced my elbow against my nose, forearm waving around like a trunk. "Gilberto! Likes to Ride! An Elephant!" I trumpeted. Teresa and Blanca exchanged worried glances. Maybe I should have said "burro," or better yet, sat at the teacher's desk pretending to grade papers like the subs I recalled from my youth. The chalk snapped as I attempted to downshift from birthday-party entertainer to self-possessed authority figure, breathlessly diagramming my highly original, wholly stupid sentence. It didn't take long. Now what? Drenched in flop sweat, I defaulted, against my better judgment, to the one thing that had almost always saved my ass in elementary school: drawing. "Look! Look, you guys," I scrawled trunk, tail, big floppy ears, "this is the elephant! And *this* is Gilberto!" I doodled the scene a couple more times, to let the humor of it sink in, then stepped back and surveyed my handiwork, as exhausted as I'd ever be, at least until having children of my own. I'd captured his hairdo, all right, but deliberately omitted his lunatic expression in favor of a generic moppet-y innocence the model most certainly did not possess. I didn't want to hurt the little nipper's feelings by shining a spotlight on his mania—not that he was exhibiting the slightest interest in his spontaneous portrait. He was too busy ripping the pages out of a classmate's library book.

I froze as the door banged open, expecting to be busted by an outraged veteran from the old-school spanker mold, but was addressed instead by a worn-looking woman in a cafeteria-worker's uniform. She leaned heavily against the metal butler's cart on which she was ferrying several plastic crates of half-pint milk cartons. "How you 'spect them to eat they lunch if they not at they desks?" she asked, though not in a critical way. I shrugged helplessly. "What's a matter, honey, ain't nobody showed up so's you can get your lunch?" I shook my head, suddenly feeling like I might burst into tears. The office worker who'd checked me in that morning hadn't said boo about how lunch was supposed to work. I'd assumed I was to escort my charges to the mess hall. Did they get anything besides milk? "All right, then," the itinerant cafeteria woman said. "I'll sit here with them till Ms. Butler shows up to spell you." Mute with gratitude, I grabbed my purse and made a beeline for the door, following the very procedure I'd have observed had she pulled a knife.

Sitting on a swing in the desolate playground, chewing the apple I had brought from home, I regarded the sinister windows of the old brick school, wondering what would happen if I took a powder. It would be so easy to walk right out of that bare cement yard and just keep going. But what about Teresa and Blanca and all the time I'd invested getting (and, I might add, passing) the TB test? No, they weren't going to shake Miss Chips that easily.

I returned from lunch resolved to rise above whatever fresh hell the little monsters directed my way with graceful indifference. I'd read *Lord of the Flies.* I knew there was no profit to be had in letting their craziness get to me. Nor was there much hope of containing the uncontrollable element. Accordingly, I passed out construction paper and glue and turned my full attention toward Blanca, Teresa, and one or two other mild souls, instructing them to get started on collages. The others could chase each other into butter for all I cared. I didn't bat an eye as Gilberto and company commando-crawled between the rows, jumping off my desk and tormenting the collage-makers by jostling their chairs. Now that the spark of progressive education had been extinguished, I had all the time in the world to gob Elmer's onto the sloppy construction-paper portraits the little girls were trying to make of such wholesome icons as Madonna and Mariah Carey. This was what drowning must be like after one gives up thrashing around and succumbs to the quiet numbness of near brain death. The roiling of small, unsupervised bodies had become strangely impersonal, like the difference between having a bad night waiting tables in the restaurant where you've worked for five months and having a bad night catering some bullshit charity dinner under a manager you'll never see again.

"You've got two seconds to get those butts in the seats, starting now!" I looked up in terror, wondering how on earth the militaristic figure striding into my classroom expected me to seize control in two seconds, when I'd spent nearly seven hours proving that I had no influence whatsoever. But watching the kids scamper toward their desks, I realized that he wasn't talking to me. "That's better. Now put your heads down on your desks until I tell you to pick them up." I watched in amazement as his bidding was carried out with absolutely zero monkey business. "They been giving you a hard time?" he inquired brusquely, eyeballing me like George C. Scott.

"Oh, no, not too bad," I dissembled unconvincingly. The visitor bore a frightening resemblance to the guy who had taught the Red Cross lifesaving course I had taken in high school, a steel-haired jarhead hell-bent on killing us both when I went to "rescue" him during my final test.

"What these kids need," he growled, "is good old-fashioned discipline! That's something they can understand, not these namby-pamby new hands-off policies, conflict resolution this, bilingual that. Isn't that right, boys and girls?"

"Yes, sir," a few meekly chorused.

Whoa! Fuck! "Are you the principal?" I whispered.

"I'm the gym teacher." He stalked to the front of the classroom. "All right, boys and girls." The children straightened up in their seats. I must admit, it was a relief to see the reins seized with so much authority. Maybe he'd take them out to the playground so I could put *my* head down on the desk. Or was I meant to accompany them when they went outside or to the gym or wherever it was he was taking them? "All right, we're going to play Thumbs Up, Seven-Up," the gym teacher announced. I was unfamiliar with the game, but a couple of kids cheered under their breath. "Be quiet. Now, who wants to be the leader?" Almost every hand went up. "You." He singled out the fourteen-looking-year-old, who walked quietly to the head of the class and raised his thumb. "Right thumb up," the gym teacher commanded, and the children, their arms folded before them on their desks, raised their right thumbs in unison. The "leader" lowered his right thumb and raised the left. "Left thumb up." Again, the gym teacher's terse order met with total compliance. Wait a minute, what? They were having gym at their desks? Even taking budget cuts into consideration, wasn't a change of venue obligatory? I seemed to recall a recent op-ed penned by a parent enraged that her child was doing calisthenics in the cafeteria. To be fair, I'd seen no evidence that this school had a cafeteria. If I were an op-ed-writing parent, I'd save my ammo for those in charge of hiring at the Board of Ed, blast them for bringing in untrained actor-types when the regular teacher called in sick. Now the leader raised both thumbs. "Seven-Up!" the gym teacher inexplicably barked.

Every thumb shot obediently up, save the ones belonging to me and him. Christ, what a miserable excuse for gym. Not only did it shirk large-muscle involvement, it made zero sense, logistically speaking. Okay, from a practical standpoint, it did keep butts in the seats, to quote the ringmaster. But why Seven-Up? Was there any connection between the Uncola and two thumbs raised, as opposed to one, in what passed for phys ed in the Chicago public school system? Why not Mr Pibb, or Diet Pepsi, or, for that matter, a simple ten-hut? Teresa was tapped to be the new leader, and the "game" continued. As much as I'd hated changing into the striped uniforms in which the other last-to-be-pickeds and I attempted to dodge the balls Jenny Pettinga and Cathy Lowry precision-whipped at our heads, I couldn't help feeling that these kids were getting the short end of it. Gilberto, especially, needed to get his ya-ya's out via genuine physical exertion. "Gilberto, you're out," the gym teacher called, blowing a whistle he pulled from his pocket. "Your leader just raised her left thumb, but look at you. You've got both of yours in the air, but it's not Seven-Up. You're out. Put your head on the desk." It was all so unfair; however, at the time I was more than happy to cede control to the hard-assed gymbarista. No matter how unenlightened, his methods were working.

I wonder if Gilberto, his cheek pressed to the desktop for the duration as other classmates went to the front to lead this inane exercise, anticipated the earsplitting report of the dismissal bell as feverishly as I did. When at long last it went off like a five-alarm fire, it signaled freedom for the both of us. His, however, was only temporary. Presumably, his teacher would soon return to put an end to his high jinks, not to mention his unauthorized spins on that elephant. My liberation was of a more permanent nature, at least as far as substitute "teaching" was concerned.

squatting nude (with arm extended)

I liked the series of short gesture drawings that kicked off class the best, because they gave me an opportunity to flex some artistic muscles of my own. Every two minutes, I got to invent a new raison d'être, a brief interior monologue to accompany the pose I struck for the dozens of eyes peering at my naked body. Over the years, a few directors had made me come up with backstories for my characters, an assignment I'd always found hokey. Hey, man, if you want a more nuanced Ophelia, cast a better actress. Randomly selecting a favorite food, a favorite color, and a name for the beloved childhood pet tragically crushed beneath the wheels of Hamlet's father's carriage as we were returning from a picnic on the blasted heath (I remember it was a sunny day in May, and the air smelled like edelweiss . . .) did not add texture to my performance. Oddly enough, I couldn't get enough of these little fake-o scenarios when I was an artist's model. Not only did they help to pass the time, they made something that was even more ephemeral than live theater seem worthy of remembering. Without some motivation to give the pose some context, it was just athleticism. With some imagination, however . . .

> NUDE WITH ARM EXTENDED. *I must stretch high to reach the rosiest apple, beckoning so invitingly from the overhanging branch.*
> KNEELING NUDE. *Drawing water from the well, I pause to admire my reflection. Soon I shall be wed!*
> SQUATTING NUDE (WITH ARM EXTENDED). *Do not be afraid, little goat! I do not wish to harm you, only feed you a few grains of corn from my open palm.*

An avowed city girl outside the confines of the studio, I became, upon disrobing, relentlessly pastoral. From all appearances, the imaginary village that provided the setting for my kneeling, squatting, and extending had yet to be visited by indoor plumbing or feminist ideals. Smiling like Mona Lisa, I froze in an attitude suggestive of hand laundry—not Woolite-ing lace bras in the bathroom sink, but the real, Old Testament, rocks-in-the-river deal. When Burt, who owned the studio, indicated that two minutes had passed, I rose to clip a dripping cotton garment to a line strung across the meadow. Two minutes later, I was back on my knees, cheerfully—if statically—scrubbing the velvet-draped surface of my modeling platform. The combination of nudity, brevity, and the wholly illusory conspired to make domestic drudgery fun, the way it was when I was eight and, over my mother's objections, selected a child-sized wooden washtub and scrub board as my souvenirs of Colonial Williamsburg.

Sadly, the time limit ensured that the richly imagined doings of my village maiden would be captured as nothing more than squiggles and lines by the would-be artists. Burt constantly berated beginners for adding little balls to the ends of their stick-figure appendages. "Her hands and feet don't matter," he'd pronounce, drawing alongside the platform on which I posed, nekkid as a jaybird. "The purpose of these opening exercises is to limber you up for her longer poses. Concentrate on the twist of the spine, the positioning of the shoulders. Look how beautifully she's got her hips canted in this one." Placing himself more than an arm's length from my body, he used his hand to trace the tilt of my pelvis as something reminiscent of a butterfly, my bikini-free bikini area standing in for its thorax.

Firefighter, police officer, doctor, ballet dancer . . . no child dreams of growing up to be an artist's model. Too bad, because it's a really easy Halloween costume. Unlike waitressing or (as I would come to find out) temping, there was never a struggle to find something clean and/or mainstream enough to wear to work. A couple of times when I mounted my platform bearing ghostly impressions of too-snug elastic, I found myself wishing that I'd put more thought into my morning underwear selection, but other than that, the wardrobe requirements were blessedly minimal. All I needed was the knee-length cotton shirt I wore on breaks and, occasionally, a tampon, its string discreetly bundled and tucked where the sun don't shine. Once, when I forgot my long shirt, Burt, who lived in the studio's back room, loaned me his plaid flannel bathrobe, which made me uncomfortable despite its reassuring grandpa smell. I try never to swap jammies with the boss, even nice ones who don't want me to have to walk around naked on my break. Luckily, I never had to hit Burt up for a tampon.

Burt's studio was not just the nicest studio in which I modeled, it was the coolest-looking work environment ever. With its graphite reek and dusty filtered light, it evoked a Paris where van Gogh bartered down his bar tab with paintings and Gauguin's thirteen-year-old mistress strolled the streets with a pet monkey on a leash. But for the students—who for some reason favored T-shirts and Reeboks over bonnets and waistcoats—it was easy to imagine the studio existing outside of twentieth-century America. Intentionally or not, Burt fostered the illusion by playing classical tapes and festooning the main floor with human skeletons. Forget my sorry bod; somebody should have drawn the studio! It was effortlessly bohemian in a way my crummy one-room apartment was not. I often dreamed that I lived there—without Burt and his brown-plaid bathrobe, I mean. Like other would-be time travelers who flatter themselves that they would have hidden entire synagogues in their basements in Nazi Germany or roared harder than Zelda in the 1920s, I liked to think that if only I hadn't been born one hundred years too late on the wrong continent, I would have been an artist's model in Montmartre, as celebrated as the most famous prostitutes of the day. I would have taken off my clothes at parties and drunk absinthe with Toulouse-Lautrec. It's a fantasy dating back to my first reading of *A Moveable Feast.* I'd always pictured myself modeling in a garret, but Burt's studio was clearly an improvement. It added a whole other layer to those two-minute gestures. The only thing more fun than impersonating a simple, sweet-natured village maiden is impersonating Kiki impersonating a simple, sweet-natured village maiden. *Do not be afrrraid, Leet-tul Got.*

My frequent, if fragmented, readings of Anaïs Nin had advanced the notion that models hold powerful sway over their artists, but Burt was too stout, gray, and aviator framed to qualify as my type. (I think the models in *Delta of Venus* aren't so much professionals as unpaid girlfriends lending a hand, kind of like me drawing flyers for Isaac's band and taping them to every lamppost in Wicker Park.) It was a relief that I didn't seem to be Burt's type, either. No way could I have withstood him describing the beautiful cant of my hips if I'd suspected him of harboring unrequited urges to ravish me on the velvet-draped platform after class. He probably enjoyed looking at naked lassies as much as any heterosexual male, but he maintained the professional detachment of a gynecologist. Besides, from what I could tell, he seemed to have some sort of longtime monogamous thing going with Peg, the wan assistant who set up the easels before class and offered words of encouragement to frustrated students when the master retired to the loftlike mezzanine, where he drank coffee with his disciples, the Handsome Brazilians.

With their dashing long manes and inverted triangular torsos, the Handsome Brazilians were more than my type, but they never came down from their balcony. Every time I jiggered myself into a pose where my head was thrown back, I got an eyeful. I wasn't looking-looking—I had Isaac, after all—just, you know, looking. They might not have turned my head if they'd been businessmen or public servants, but they were—yeah, baby—*artists,* the most serious of Burt's serious students. Anyone who could ante up fifteen bucks per session could attend the open-session classes starring me, though these casual pupils' frequent lack of discipline and/or ability seemed to leave cold the man whose rent they were paying. Burt's darlings were his advanced students, whom he subjected to a course of instruction almost medieval in its rigor. Before he allowed them to so much as touch charcoal to paper, they had to spend an entire year sculpting life-sized human skeletons out of oily gray clay. "Otherwise, they'll never truly understand the body as a three-dimensional form," Burt told me with a small, nicotine-stained smile. If an open-session attendee had inquired as to the purpose of the skeleton-sculpting, his answer would have been brusque to the point of rudeness, but me he dealt with fondly, sort of like the mascot who's as much a part of the team as the quarterback. I guess it would have been impolitic to imply that the model is incapable of understanding the body as a three-dimensional form until she's re-created its bony processes in gray Play-Doh. I was glad to be exempted, but I also revered Burt's approach, figuring that anyone capable of toughing out that first year had both the commitment and the capacity for deprivation shown by all serious artists (except for Jeff Koons) (and Damien Hirst) (who, though he may saw cows in half and display their cross-sectioned carcasses at the Guggenheim, has never sculpted a cow skeleton in gray clay or anything else, to the best of my admittedly spotty knowledge). (Like many artist's models, I like to pretend I know a lot about art.)

Few of the advanced candidates made it through their first year. Out of the corner of my eye, I once saw a woman who'd spent the better part of two months fashioning a pelvis from scratch angrily squash the thing into a nondescript wad. "That's it," she spat. "I quit! My sanity's worth more than some shitty bone." On her way out, she paused to fire a parting shot. "You know, all I ever wanted was to paint gardens like Monet!"

"You came to the wrong place," Burt observed as the door slammed, before leaning over the balcony rail to ask Peg if the pelvis-woman's tuition check had cleared. The open-session attendees who had witnessed this meltdown took a break from sketching me to buzz among themselves, but the

Handsome Brazilians remained implacable. Both of them had been toiling on their skeletons for more than five years, which may have explained why they got to hang around on the mezzanine drinking coffee, while below them the pay-as-you-go, open-session rabble scratched away at their pads and advanced students who had yet to reach the one-year mark molded scapulae and spinal columns on top of chest-high wheeled platforms. Occasionally, one of the Handsome Brazilians might use his thumb to smooth out a rib, but mainly it seemed like they were there solely to put their handsome heads together over Burt's many art books, whispering in Portuguese and providing me with eye candy.

Although I knew their names, we never spoke—unless you count the time I was twenty minutes late to class and Burt designated Roberto to pinch-hit in my absence. I had expected to find the students making do with a bowl of fruit or something. The sight of Handsome Roberto straddling the platform in his birthday suit brought me to a dead halt, the cockamamie story I had invented to explain my tardiness dying on my lips. He looked like an Aztec warrior, petrified mid-crouch. The profile he offered was manly and fierce, though his hair, free of its customary rubber band, rippled softly down his bare back. His straining quadriceps could not have been more clearly delineated had he been flayed. I couldn't help but note that his spear was exceptionally long. "God, do *I* look that naked?" I wondered as Roberto, spying me among the easels, abruptly abandoned his pose and pulled on Burt's bathrobe.

"Roberto, man, you really saved my ass," I said, unconsciously reaching for the faintly bitch-flavored camaraderie one finds in restaurant kitchens and at corporate Xerox machines. "The El sat in the tunnel for like half an hour and before that, my alarm clock didn't—"

"Eet ees nothing," he replied, stalking to the bathroom to re-robe.

My tardiness had given us something in common, but I could never bring myself to ask him whether he had prior experience as a model, let alone whether he invented little stories to give an extra dimension to his poses. *You are a worthy opponent, Brother Jaguar, but soon you shall taste the long shaft of my spear . . . .*

Once the two-minute gestures I loved so well had the students sufficiently loose, I moved, none too keenly, into longer poses. Anyone who's ever attempted to empty her mind (or look groovy) via meditation can attest that after five minutes, the legs lose all sensation. At the seven-minute mark, the sitter (stander, kneeler . . .) begins to have some insight into what it must feel like to withstand the rack. Finding the physical position least likely to simulate torture was a process of trial and error. It seemed to me the best all-around bet was to lie on the floor. I could quell my monkey mind with a little nap-a-roo while the students drew for as long as they liked, filling in eyelashes and freckles until their hands curled. The recumbent position had the added advantage of taking ten pounds off my equatorial problem area. The first time I attempted this maneuver, though, a bunch of back-row spoilsports complained that they couldn't *see* me. Wearily, I pushed myself into a standing pose, my front leg bearing all of my weight as I beckoned, yet again, to the timid but hungry goat—always a crowd-pleaser.

"Are you sure you're okay to hold that for twenty minutes?" Peg asked as the students' charcoals went into action. I considered. Choosing to hold one's arm parallel to the floor for the duration of a long pose is showy but fraught with peril, the model's equivalent of Evel Knievel jumping his motorcycle over fifteen flaming Volkswagens. What starts as a mild tingle running from fingertips to biceps can proceed to excruciating, oh-my-god-it-feels-like-they're-being-lopped-off-with-an-ax panic in the blink of an eye. Conceding that it might not be such a bad idea to humor Peg on this one, I dropped the arm and started casting about for something less challenging.

"But I'd already started to draw her that way," an elderly woman in a cast-off dental hygienist's smock carped, as the other students flipped to fresh pages.

"Better watch your mouth, Lady," I thought to myself, hoping that one day the old bat might wander into a restaurant and wind up seated in my section.

"I often find a fresh start to be helpful," Peg soothed, as she pulled a stub of graphite from her pocket to layer some corrective handiwork over what little the complainer had managed to draw. "Now take a good look at her breasts. See how they sort of slope downward, like this? You've made them way too round . . . ."

The worst pose I ever got myself into appeared to be the most innocuous: feet spaced a comfortable hips' width apart, hands clasped loosely behind my back. In an attempt to lend some mystery to the straightforward, I held my head cocked slightly to the left, chin approaching clavicle, as if lost in thought. Had this been a quickie gesture drawing, I might have committed to my craft fully and spent the entire time contemplating the great feast we would prepare when threshing time was done, but that simple-peasant shit's shelf life maxed out at two minutes. I couldn't see the Handsome Brazilians from that angle, but in a feat of pre-pose cunning, I'd deposited my newspaper on the side of my platform. Even with my contacts in, I had little hope of deciphering individual words from that distance, but

I figured I had little better to do than try. Earlier in the week, that very paper had published an article about a doctor who restored poor vision through a series of ocular exercises and, more importantly, the patient's willingness to keep his or her eyes trained on an object until it "naturally" came into focus. If I couldn't see well enough to read the newspaper folded on the platform, at least I could divert myself by achieving twenty-twenty vision. What I really wanted, of course, was a book, even more passionately than I had longed for one in *Native Americans of the Pacific Northwest.* Western art abounds with images of reading women, some of them naked, but I felt it would be unprofessional of me to ask Burt if I could tote Margaret Atwood onto the platform with me. Instant gratification probably doesn't hold much water for a guy who makes paying students sculpt bones for months on end. I couldn't risk losing face with him by whining about the tedium of standing around naked for twenty dollars an hour. I imagined him discussing such a request with his artist friends the way society matrons allegedly compare notes on "the help." *Say yes to the book, and next they'll want to know is it okay if they bring their vibrators up so they won't get bored.*

The ophthalmologic experiment was not going well, which meant that I'd have to anchor my sanity to my same old tatters of memories—larded with scraps of show tunes and bursts of paranoia about being late to auditions and forgetting to feed a vacationing neighbor's fish—in other words, the sort of meaningless chatter that plagues insomniacs at four in the morning. I even had my own version of counting sheep, in which I catalogued everything I could see without turning my head. Usually this went something like: *box of graphite, box of graphite, open box of graphite, rolled-up poster, stack of folded muslin, plaster cast of human foot, art book, art book, art book, skull, white coffee cup.* That was the north wall. The Handsome Brazilians' lair was much more interesting but certain to cause a crick in the neck. I tried not to look at the students, because I found myself resenting them for indulging in a hobby while I had to stand around bored. I wonder if peep-show girls feel the same way about the people facing them. Friends who can't imagine themselves taking off their clothes for money think that artist's models spend their whole time on the platform thinking, "Oh my god, I'm naked, I'm naked, I'm naked," which in truth is about as likely as thinking, "Oh my god, I have pierced ears, I have pierced ears, I have pierced ears." The novelty wears off almost immediately. And though you may relieve yourself of a minute or two by coming up with the perfect retort to the popular girl who called you a social retard in seventh grade, eventually you return to dully cataloguing the flotsam along the north wall, because what else are you going to do? Watch the clock? That way madness lies.

Initially, the problem with the innocuous pose was that the downward angling of my head made for such slim visual pickings that the boxes of graphite seemed like a Mardi Gras float in comparison. *Black velvet platform edge, blurry newspaper, linoleum, aluminum easel legs, white running shoes, blue running shoes, brown vinyl . . . oh Christ, I'm suffocating! I can't swallow! Feels like someone's pressing a gun into the base of my skull! Don't shoot! Oh Christ, oh Jesus, what did they say about Jesus, being pounded into the cross isn't what killed him, he died because he was too weak to lift his head, so he suffocated. Oh shit, why did I put my head down like Jesus's? So thirsty! No shade! Big crowd of Romans with easels at the base of the cross! Somebody take me down off this thing! Can't breathe!* With a strangulated croak, I fell to my hands and knees a good ten minutes before the pose was scheduled to end. "Sorry, Peg, I got dizzy," I gasped, not caring that my breasts dangled like udders or that my genitals were presenting themselves to the students with bovine frankness.

After the crucifixion incident, I was permitted to lean on a broomstick for anything slated to go longer than five minutes, on the theory that a third leg might prevent me from keeling over. I also adjusted my pose so that if anyone had balanced a carpenter's level atop my head, I guarantee the air bubble would have lined up exactly as it was supposed to in the little glass pane. Sometimes you don't want to get back on that horse, know what I mean?

"Not her again," one of the open-session students groused as I mounted the platform a few weeks after I had disgraced myself. He grasped an imaginary staff, stiffened his body, and frowned dead ahead.

"Would you care to take your clothes off and show us how it's done?" Burt inquired so coldly I think my nipples may have stiffened.

"No thanks," the cutup smirked. "*I* have a Ph.D."

In what? Not taking his clothes off in public? Asshololology? I was a model so I was stupid, was that it? "You dickhead," I should have shouted, "I'll have you know I have a bachelor's degree in . . . in . . . theater . . . ."

You know, perhaps maintaining my dignity through silence *was* the right choice.

i hate mondays

I didn't even come close to passing the typing test, but thanks to a friend from acting class who had pull at the temp agency, I, too, found myself scrounging for business attire in my size-4 roommate's closet. Semi-disguised in her khaki blazer and some rumpled Salvation Army purchases, I joined the early-morning white-collar hordes streaming up the subway stairs, bound for buildings that had separate elevator banks for the highest floors. At first it seemed exotic, choosing which subterranean eatery would get my luncheon business, greeting the security guards with the familiarity of a career-track climber, searching through the drawers of whomever I was replacing in quest of BreathSavers or other tasty treats. Ultimately, though, I must say that temping is like being the blind date of someone you'd never want to hang out with, at a party where everybody's known everybody else since kindergarten, where the food's bad and runs out early.

On my first assignment, I forgot to bring a book, or even a newspaper. I brought my floppy disk, but there was no computer on which to work on what I liked to think of as my yet-to-be-published collected poems. The desk drawers were locked. Not counting me and the pink message pad, the only thing in the reception area that wasn't an office-approved shade of "battleship," "pearl," "charcoal," or "ash" was a Sears Portrait Studio photograph of a pug-nosed toddler in a lavender sweatshirt with a unicorn decal. I hadn't seen a soul since the woman from human resources had cast a critical eye at my outfit and led me to this chamber. With no sense of my coordinates, I felt a bit like Alice in a dreary, nearly deserted Wonderland, though I doubt I would have followed a white rabbit should one have materialized. I didn't want to wind up lost in a maze of identical gray "areas," the framed toddler my only landmark. As long as I didn't go in search of lunch or the bathroom, I could make my way back to the elevator at five. Speaking of which, I wondered who would sign my timecard at the end of the day, assuming that the minutes were indeed crawling forward and not suspended in an indefinite stasis. Maybe if I dialed zero, the operator could tell me what to do. God, what I wouldn't have given for a candy striper to come by with a cart of magazines or something . . . or even a visit from my old Moondancer nemesis, Chet! Anything to relieve the climate-controlled boredom. Then, without the slightest warning, the rectangular phone lit up like a malevolent, self-determining robot and started emitting an insistent, electronic warble. I was being ambushed! I fumbled the receiver, punched the wrong line button, and dropped my message pad, instinctively displaying the professionalism for which we temps are known and justly celebrated.

"Hello?" I gasped, having blanked on the name of the law firm whose phones I was answering. The caller was so livid at this generic greeting, I had a moment of terror that he might be one of the five partners. But no, he was just one of the many Very Important A-holes I was to encounter telephonically throughout my career as a temp.

"Tom Barker," he barked.

"Just one moment, sir," I cowered, yanking again on the locked drawer in a fruitless attempt to rustle up a company manifest. "Uh, do you know the extension, Mr. Barker?"

"No," and here the words "you idiot" were tacitly understood on both sides, "I'm *calling* for Barker!"

"Yes, of course, I'm so sorry. Just let me try that extension for you." I jabbed the hold button and hyperventilated for a moment. There were a couple of closed doors visible down the hallway, and beyond that I knew not what. Think! Think! Taking a deep breath, I reconnected to the V.I.A-hole. "I'm sorry, sir, Mr. Barker has stepped out of his office. May I take a message?"

"I'm *returning* his call. He *just* called me. So *how* could he have stepped *out* of his office?" Despite my scrabbling-lab-rat frame of mind, I scrounged up some healthy resentment for this Mr. Not-Barker, who clearly plowed through his Very Important Days with nary a thought for the service-industry personnel left flattened in his wake. In all likelihood, he probably had his own secretary mailing off an application to Northwestern University's theater department on behalf of his high school–age daughter. The injustice!

"I don't know, sir, but I just rang his line and nobody answered. Do you want me to try him ag—"

"Just tell him Bob Frank returned his call," the V.I.A-hole shouted and hung up with a bang. I leaned my forehead on the edge of the desk and stared at a run in my just-purchased No

Nonsenses. When I sat up, I had forgotten whom the V.I.A-hole had been calling for.

Once I'd cut my teeth on a string of one- and two-day assignments, the big bananas at my agency rewarded me with a longer-term post, replacing a vacationing receptionist. "You'll like this one," one of the bananas intimated as I copied down the address for yet another towering corporate headquarters. "They're a lot of fun!" Fun, I was to discover, signified an office decorated nearly exclusively in Garfield—you know, the testicle-eyed striped cat addicted to naps and lasagna. This assignment had an open floor plan: six receptionists seated in a communal area so brightly lit with overhead fluorescents, even someone with my poor eyesight could read the "funny" Monday-related slogans tacked to the dividers behind nearby desks. There were Garfield snow globes, Garfield mugs, little spring-and-suction-cup Garfields mounted to the top of computer monitors. God, how I loathed King World Features, or whatever syndicate was responsible for peddling this hairy orange fucker as a symbol of anarchy. My rabble was roused thinking of all the worthier things my hard-working neighbors could have squandered their paychecks on: Butthole Surfers T-shirts, Manic Panic hair color, union dues. I wanted them to prove their Monday hatred by setting the wastebaskets aflame or shouting, "Chuck this, Farlie!" midway through a dictation session. Instead, they settled for flaunting Garfield's watered-down defiance as their own, sipping from I HATE MONDAY mugs right in front of the boss on, get this, a Monday!

The divider behind my own temporary desk boasted a depressingly vast collection of round Garfield campaign-style buttons. I wondered if their owner ever wore them. One of the other receptionists met with great hilarity when she came in one morning sporting a pair of deelybobbers, those little headband-mounted novelty antennae, tipped with twin Garfield heads. She slipped them off unbidden when one of her male bosses arrived. Although I disliked Garfield with an intensity I usually reserve for actual humans—high-salaried businesspeople who regard the arts as the province of weirdos, say—I felt no animosity toward the jolly permanent receptionists. Okay, except for Joanne, the oldest of the bunch, whose desk abutted mine and who always behaved as if I was some sort of interloper horning in on their private Garfieldklatsch. She was sort of prideful and grumpy, indignant when one of her superiors caught an error in something she had typed. A control freak in a pastel Lane Bryant pantsuit, Joanne eavesdropped on idle office chatter in order to correct her colleagues. Her strongly held opinions on everything from baby-shower gifts to the menu at T.G.I. Friday's often took the form of hindsight critique. When Marci showed off the new cubic zirconia she'd bought at Sears, Joanne clucked that Kohl's had the exact same pendant for five dollars less. "Why on earth would you and Bob go to Red Lobster on a Tuesday?" she interrupted a colleague who was describing her tenth anniversary dinner. "Their all-you-can-eat surf and turf special is on Thursday!" The day before the woman I was covering for was due back from sunny Florida, one of the other "gals" was celebrating her birthday. Whenever someone from another floor passed through our area, Joanne made sure to draw his or her attention to the helium-filled Mylar Garfield head tethered to the birthday girl's chair. "Isn't that balloon the biggest stitch you ever saw?" she would ask in a challenging tone of voice. "I'm the one who gave that to her."

I wanted to get right up in her face, shake her by the shoulders, and shout, "Woman, that's not something to be proud of!"

Instead, I just helped myself to one more cough drop from the true occupant's desk drawer, feeling strangely embarrassed that I hadn't known about the occasion with enough advance notice to swing by the basement-level card kiosk. I felt like maybe if it had been my birthday, the birthday girl would have gotten the others to chip in for a Garfield card with my name on it. Or somebody's name. When I was gathering my stuff together at five o'clock, she took a moment from her own special day to acknowledge my leave-taking. "Good luck, Pam," she called. "I'll be looking for your name in lights!"

Someday, I'm sure, someone named Pam is going to be a great, big, juicy star.

I gave the big pharmaceutical firm high marks because of the chair, a highly engineered butt-cuddler upholstered in rich-smelling leather. It was far more comfortable than any of the jet trash with which my roommates and I had furnished our apartment. It tilted and adjusted and supported my lumbar region as capably as it molded to the particulars of my own personal heiner. I could, I decided, get very used to spending eight hours a day in such a chair. Yet at the end of the day, the temp agency's biggest banana called to tell me that the assignment I'd expected to last at least a couple of weeks was to be terminated effective immediately. My chair! "We need to talk," she said. "Are you wearing pantyhose?"

I'd been taught to blow a whistle in the receiver, hang up, and phone the police in response to such a question, but given the circumstances, I had a hunch why she was asking. "Yes," I lied. "I mean, no. I mean, I was, but I got a big run in them on my way to work, and I didn't think they'd want me to be walking around looking like I had a big ladder on my leg." I caressed my bare calves, frantically dissembling in an attempt to cover my ass from every conceivable angle. "I meant to go out and get another pair on my lunch break, but then it got so busy that I didn't take lunch until three, and by then, I forgot. And also, it turns out, I only had enough money for a sandwich."

"All right, well, we'll see what we can get you for tomorrow, then. But for the future, you might want to start keeping a bottle of clear nail polish in your bag, along with a spare pair of nylons just in case."

"Absolutely," I promised.

Later, my friend from acting class told me that I'd been reclassified from FOA to not-FOA. I was unfamiliar with the term. "Front Office Appearance," she explained, as gently as possible.

I spent nearly six weeks with the sepulchral Mr. Lyman, whom I regarded as an executive version of a fellow FOA demotee, although there was nothing amiss about his grooming. On the contrary, he was like something from another age, a relic. The other execs, ruddy-cheeked lads with freshly minted wedding bands and brand-new mortgages, were not much older than I. They played racquetball on their lunch hours and razzed the secretaries, all of whom called them by their first names. It was eerie how many of them were named Chip. To a man, they enjoyed the top-rated sitcoms of the day, windsurfing on Lake Michigan, and all-inclusive, couples-only vacation packages in tropical locales.

"So, Anna, what do you do for fun?" one of the Chips inquired, leaning casually on my desk. "When you're not working, I mean."

"Uh, I'm an actor," I said, keeping my eyes locked on his as I stealthily palmed the used paperback edition of *One Flew over the Cuckoo's Nest* that I'd been reading under a stack of interoffice envelopes.

"What, like television?" he asked, cocking his handsome, blow-dried head in a gesture he seemed to think passed for curiosity. I could just imagine him sitting through some corporate-training seminar on how to put a prospective candidate at ease. It was having the opposite effect on me. I had a hunch that Mr. Lyman would not be pleased to discover one of the young bucks lolling about on his secretary's desk.

"Uh, no, not TV," I said, casting a nervous glance at Mr. Lyman's door. "Theater, actually."

"Whoa, seriously? Like what, Shakespeare and all of that?" I nodded, having appeared several years earlier as Ophelia in an abbreviated five-person *Hamlet* that toured suburban high schools out near the mall where I'd made such a splash as Bert. "That's wild!" He asked if I was in a play now. I nodded again. He asked if I had a flyer. I nodded again, having surreptitiously run off five hundred of them while Mr. Lyman was in a meeting. He folded the one I gave him into quarters and slipped it into his jacket's interior pocket, alleging that he thought it would be fun to try to get a whole gang from the office together to go see the show. I silently prayed that he would not, that some unseen valve would prevent him from entering my world the way I had entered his. "So, how do you like working for old Winky?" Chip must have taken what felt to me like a grimace as a smile of collusion. Before I could formulate a noncommittal reply, he was blinking to beat the band in spasmodic parody of Mr. Lyman's facial tic. Mr. Lyman's hands and head shook, too, not Katharine Hepburn–bad, but noticeably enough that I assumed it was some sort of neurological ailment.

"I thought his first name was Robert," I said, gallantly

deciding that this was one baited hook I could allow myself the luxury of refusing to bite.

"Robert, right, but we call him 'Winky' because of, you know." Again with the eyes.

The intercom buzzed. "Miss Halliday, I wonder if you have any experience replacing the self-correcting ribbons," an elderly voice enunciated with painfully outmoded diction. "My typewriter seems to be giving me some trouble."

"Yes, of course, Mr. Lyman, I'll be right there," I replied, feeling efficient and loyal and kind of like Barbara Stanwyck as I rose to my feet without another glance in Chip's direction. Mr. Lyman awaited me at his desk, his hands inky from grappling with several yards of typewriter ribbon. "Oh dear, you're not supposed to pull it out of its cartridge like that," I said. I used an interoffice envelope to scrape the tangled remains into the trash, feeling very glad that Chip hadn't witnessed this pathetic scene. I'll bet he hadn't typed a word since he turned in his business school thesis, the twerp. "Whatever you're working on, I can type it up for you out front," I offered, wondering if perhaps he was going a bit soft upstairs to attempt these menial secretarial skills on his own. I reached for the steno pad covered in Mr. L's messy penmanship.

"I'm afraid it's of a personal nature," he snapped, snatching the pad up before I could see what was written on it. My flesh crawled as I imagined a letter to *Penthouse* Forum . . .

> *My secretary writhed with pleasure atop the desk as my eight and a half executive inches plunged into the creamy slot in her torn nylons . . . .*

The horror.

"You know how to do tables in Database, right?" the boss lady asked, as she handed me a manila folder full of sales reports that I'd been brought in to squish together or spin into gold or something or other before sunrise.

"Yes," I lied, after a moment's hesitation. Like the previous postings' ubiquitous Chips, she and I were close enough in age to be considered peers. I didn't want her to think me incapable, though in retrospect, it seems a battle lost before it could begin. Left to my own devices, I could barely figure out which key would open up the new document I was supposedly creating. As soon as the boss lady returned to her office, I placed the first of many panicked sotto voce phone calls to Rumpelstiltskin, otherwise known as my friend from acting class. It took me all day, but by skipping lunch and eschewing the table commands my friend had done her best to tutor me in in favor of the tab key, I managed to scrape the assignment together. By the time I finally hit "print," I was little more than a quivering bundle of exposed nerves, convinced that computers had been invented to make me feel bad about myself. Why was I so goddamned warped? Why couldn't I whip out spreadsheets and flow charts and enjoy Garfield's excesses like the rest of the workforce? How come I hated T.G.I. Friday's and situation comedies? My interest in theater and thrift stores rendered me unfit to function in this society. I was like some sort of hemophiliac royal whiling my days away in an ivory tower, translating poetry into archaic languages, soon to be slaughtered in the peasant uprising. Also, I'd bagged out on the Introduction to Computers course I'd enrolled in in college when a spot unexpectedly opened in Performative Interpretation of African Literature.

The boss lady was not pleased. "You know, this sort of project really shouldn't take more than an hour," she sniffed when I knocked on her open door.

"Yeah, it's just that I'm accustomed to working on a different version of the program," I hedged. "It's the same, but different."

"What's this? Oh no. Oh no, no, no," she moaned, beginning to tug on her bangs as she looked over the sheet. "I told you to separate these out by region, not monthly grosses. I told Antwerp I'd fax this through by 6 AM their time! What have you done? Do you have any idea how screwed I am?"

I don't imagine it would have made her feel much better if I had answered yes.

I spent eight hours in a windowless cubicle doing nothing but ripping the perforated margins off a green-and-beige striped printout taller than a two-drawer filing cabinet and didn't mind it a bit, because the last few nights had been spent in the arms of a ponytailed bartender who smoked clove cigarettes and played with my fingers when we went out for pancakes at two o'clock in the afternoon. His company went a long way toward salving the emotional wounds I'd suffered when Isaac ditched me for that nasty bottle-meddler, Drake-Ann. Wylie was nineteen years old. I was so chafed I could barely stand. I fancied that the suits with whom I shared the elevator to the twenty-sixth floor could tell. The events of the weekend seemed only more deliciously romantic when considered in the fluorescent light of the corporate setting.

It all came to a head when, somehow, I wound up at Amoco on the brink of the Gulf War. I'd knocked around various floors for six weeks before being moved into an open-ended assignment in Foreign Acquisitions. My tasks were light enough that I had plenty of time to write long letters and draw flyers for upcoming shows. The man whose phones I was responsible for answering seemed a decent enough guy. He had family photographs displayed on his credenza, and whenever he asked me to type something, he did so with a please and a thank you. Thank Christ he never required any tables in Database. Several times he mentioned how pleased he was with my work. Plus, there was a big, out-of-the-way cabinet well stocked with office supplies, which allowed me to play Robin Hood on behalf of our impoverished theater company, which ran through Post-its, tape, and Sharpie markers at an alarming rate. I even managed to snitch a wall-sized map of the world, which I hung on my living room wall after scissoring away the Amoco logo marring the bottom corner.

Not a bad gig at all, except for the increasingly urgent phone calls from Iraq and Saudi Arabia. When I was a backpacking budget traveler, the Middle East had never held much allure for me. I preferred Thailand's groovy Buddhism, Indonesia's gamelan, the gorillas and game preserves of East Africa. Now the first President Bush had done what friends who'd traversed Jordan on camel-back could not—he'd made the Middle East come alive for me as something more than a destination I'd never hankered to visit.

"Tell him I'm in a meeting," my boss would say every time I announced a call from a country in the news.

"Still?" the caller would wail, dismayed to be receiving the same flimsy excuse on his sixth call of the day that he had on his first. "Listen, it's dire that I speak to him at some point in the very near future." After a couple of dozen calls, I could recognize voices and even remember telephone numbers, complete with country code. Dead opposed to what I, like most low-budget temping actors, believed would be a war waged on behalf of corporate oil interests, I still rooted for these guys to get through to the boss, any boss. Their words weren't so different from the V.I.A-holes, but tonally, they were worlds apart. The V.I.A-holes were blunt and entitled, impervious to the notion that even a lowly message-taker might be deserving of courtesy. When these foreign-outpost guys said it was dire that they get through, they sounded like they were on the verge of tears. They were begging me, but my hands were tied. I suddenly realized what must have been going down in all those meetings I had welcomed as opportunities to graze at the all-you-can-sneak office-supply bar. The evil corporate giant that had lured these pathetic overseas callers into this mess with stock options and handsome vacation packages was instructing its top brass to turn a deaf ear. What could I do to help? Well, the first thing, obviously, was to paint our theater company's draft-age male intern red several nights a week before an audience numbering in the dozens. After that, I wasn't sure. I did have access to the corporate directory . . . .

"I'm afraid I don't quite understand what you mean," the big banana from the temp agency said when I called to give her the news.

"Because of my political beliefs," I repeated, "I can't in good conscience work for *Amoco* if we're going to *war* in the *Persian Gulf*." This was met with the sort of complete silence theater folk refer to onomatopoeically as "cricket, cricket." "I can no longer . . . work . . . for Am-o-co."

"But dear, you don't work for Amoco. You work for us!" She seemed quite happy to shoulder the moral burden. "Besides, Amoco loves you. Everyone I've spoken to there has given you very high marks." Marks? I wasn't sure if she was being rhetorical, or if I should send my friend from acting class off on another archaeological dig through my file. "Look, whatever you might do or think in your off-hours is your own private business." I looked at the red paint under my fingernails. Definitely not FOA. I had to admit they had my number there.

"But one rule we must ask all our temps to abide by is that they make themselves available for any assignment that falls within their skill set, whatever or wherever that assignment may be. It's simple professionalism, really."

("Cricket, cricket.")

The big banana heaved an elaborate, disappointed sigh. "All right, you're putting us in a very difficult position, but we'll see if we can find something else for you to do."

I'm still waiting for that call.

smells like teen chorus girls

My first assignment was to curry close to a hundred Easter bunny suits in preparation for the upcoming holiday. The cheap models didn't give me much trouble. Gladys had laundered the one-piece terry-cloth jammies as they were returned the previous April, so I started by burrowing through a giant file drawer labeled ANIMAL MITTS, making white pairs of approximately the same size, which I clipped to each suit's left sleeve. I checked the oversized heads for dings or tears in the eye netting, making repairs as needed with poster paint and duct tape. Although everything in our vast inventory had been "designed" by Dick Kratt, Showstopper Costumes' exceedingly bitchy, quick-to-find-fault boss, I noted that these cheap bunnies were identical to the suit my grandfather had donned to entertain at my fourth birthday party. Grampy's skipping and waving proved a huge hit with my guests as we scrambled around the backyard in pastel dress coats, bonnets, and white gloves, hunting the candy my mother had tucked, none too discreetly, into the forked branches of the forsythia. Debbie Graf and Becky May fell particular prey to the illusion created by that zippered body and immobile, buck-toothed grin. It was family lore how Grampy managed to pull his head back on just seconds before Debbie and Becky burst into my parents' bedroom, following the bunny as he sought relief from the nauseating heat exhaustion I can personally attest is the bane of all full-body mascots. I reveled in the delicious sense of superiority I felt over Debbie and Becky for believing that my costumed grandfather was the real deal. I knew that the real Easter bunny was something like a god. His head would be covered in soft fur, not painted papier-mâché that sounded hollow when thumped. He would look every bit as real as Bert had.

Fluffer was like a god—fur, head to toe. His ears were lined with pink satin, and his tail was a luxurious puff the size of a toilet lid. Several dozen Fluffers awaited my attentions, once the el cheapos were presentable. Fluffer rented for more than double the price of his down-market terry-cloth cousin, more still if the customer sprang for his floppy white fur feet. The feet ensured that the creature stumbling around the church's side yard after Sunday school was a seven-foot anthropomorphic rabbit, not just some asshole in the assistant rector's Florsheims.

Oddly enough, we didn't rent a single resurrected Christ suit. Having devoted several eight-hour shifts to filthy Fluffer feet, I was all for dispensing with the secular elements that have sprung up around Easter. Such an easy costume to throw together, Jesus: a rough cotton shift with a rope belt, an unstyled brown wig . . . then send 'em to the sales department for spirit gum and a beard.

Instead, I found myself tugging a wire brush through all sorts of nasty, hardened clumps that had escaped the mandatory and apparently lax dry cleaning the costumes had been given the previous April. The feet hadn't been dry-cleaned at all, just chucked into a burlap sack as they were returned. By the third morning, this atheist had resorted to prayer, begging for just one Fluffer whose condition bespoke a rental period padding quietly around a carpeted, refreshment-free drawing room. Maybe if I'd been raised Pentecostal. The best the Episcopal approach yielded was a lot of vigorous outdoor activity in the rain. Given how easy it is to step in dog shit under normal conditions, just imagine what starts sticking to you when the mesh-covered slot located several inches away from your eyes renders you legally blind.

"Mmm, yummy," Steven, one of two veteran stylists, commented, watching me tear loose a scarab of crushed, hardened jellybean. "Don't worry, it gets worse," he called as he trundled away beneath an armload of ball gowns for a suburban production of *La Traviata.*

"Halloween," the other stylist, Laverne, clarified, huffing a bit as she hoisted her three hundred pounds up a rolling metal staircase toward a drawer that contained nothing but lacey jabots.

From where I sat, those drawers seemed like a floor-to-ceiling treasure chest. I wanted off Easter bunny detail so I could plunder their fabulous contents. I was familiar with all the terminology, thanks to a favorite professor in college, a costume designer who wore cravats with sweater vests and spent entire classes reading aloud from the *New York Times'* obituary page. The air around Virgil was further rarefied by his insistence that we commit hundreds of archaic apparel-related terms to heart: jabots, four-in-hands, lorgnettes, bell toppers, armistice blouses, frock coats, opera pumps, sack suits, panniers, the difference between knickers and plus-fours. In the theatrical real world, someone who knows how to construct one of those lacy things Captain Hook wears at his throat is usually prized above an educated idiot who merely knows what it's called, but my vocabulary so dazzled Dick Kratt that he overlooked the shaky seam I ran through the Singer at the sewing portion of my interview. When he called to tell me the job was mine, I rejoiced, imagining that unlimited access to drawers filled with flapper plumes, mantillas, fur stoles, and a near-endless supply of gloves classified by color and length would inevitably result in frequent and spirited bouts of dress-up. The reality of the situation was hard to swallow. Just as I was on the verge of quitting, I racked my last Fluffer and got the go-ahead to help Steven "pull" a show.

Although we were always open for walk-ins, the bulk of our business came from high schools and community-theater groups as far away as Texas. We had plots for frequently produced chestnuts like *Hello, Dolly!* and *The Music Man*, as well as dead wood like *Finian's Rainbow* and *Destry Rides Again.* The process went something like this: After auditions had been held, the director sent us the cast's measurements. One of the "rental stylists" (Steven, Laverne, or, in the case of a particularly ill-starred production, me) would be dispatched to the vast storage area to pull costumes for each actor. Pending Dick Kratt's approval, Latrelle and Candelaria, assisted by Steven, Laverne, and, have pity, me, altered the garments to fit. Then the rental stylist in charge of the show packed the whole shebang into boxes with a whole host of accessories and shipped them out via UPS in time for the first dress rehearsal. The renter held on to the costumes for the duration of the run, usually no more than a couple of weekends. After the final curtain, the entire "collection" was stuffed back in the boxes to be shipped back to us, unlaundered. More on that later.

Steven was more amused than irritated by my newbie enthusiasm. He was a poster boy for employee dissatisfaction. He hated Dick Kratt, hated our "tacky" stock, hated all major holidays, and hated most musical theater, but his loathing was not unbecoming, because he expressed it cheerfully enough and because he was exceedingly good at what he did. I'd heard him conferring with Laverne before we started pulling *Oklahoma!*, my maiden voyage through storage. "They're saving money by having the cowboys provide their own jeans, so it's just hats, boots, and plaid shirts for the boys. One of them has size thirteen feet, but I think it's do-able. The girls are nothing special. One of them claims to be allergic to polyester, la-di-da. The biggest problem that I can foresee is their Ado Annie." Laverne, peering over his shoulder at the measurement sheet, gave a low whistle. "She's a big girl," Steven agreed, crinkling his pug nose for the benefit of his unembarrassed, queen-sized colleague. "That *Carousel* we had out in Palatine just came back from the cleaners, which is good because they had a big girl, too. Candelaria had to let the seams all the way out on the hideous dotted Swiss, remember? I guess we can squeeze her into that for the first act and do a skirt and blouse for the wedding, tarted up with that big blue cameo and some sort of frou-frou hat to distinguish her from Aunt Eller, but that leaves the box social. Hmm. I noticed you've got both the purple and the yellow Cowbelles on hold . . . ."

"Take the purple. It's bigger," Laverne offered immediately. "I got them out for someone who phoned in about a masquerade ball. Wanna bet me a hundred that she never shows?"

"It'd be her loss if she did. Thanks for the purple. You ready?" he asked, turning to me. Beneath the black beret he wore at all times, his tiny eyes glinted with faux excitement. He tossed me a measuring tape, and we headed to the back, swinging by the hold rack to retrieve a gigantic lavender dress dripping with bows, plastic flowers, and synthetic lace. "Pretty," Steven declared, sticking his tongue between his teeth.

"This is for Ado Annie?" I asked, glad to grasp any straw that could make me seem like a professional, someone who knew what was what.

"Well, not originally," he said, holding aside the heavy plastic flaps that separated the climate-controlled work area from the alternately freezing or sweltering storage area. "Dick designed these for the Bar Show, you know, that annual thing where every lawyer in town gets drunk, gets dressed, and puts on skits?" Steven shuddered with something I can only call gallows appreciation. "They've always got a drag number, right, and last year it was four big, beefy guys dressed up like Scarlett O'Hara. Get it? Southern belles? Cowbelles?" He led me over to a pipe where the lavender dress's sisters stretched the dry cleaner's plastic wrappings to capacity. "I wish there was some way we could do her in the yellow," he sighed, skinning back the plastic on what looked like a lace-trimmed inflatable raft, the kind that takes tourists down the Colorado River four at a time. "It looks a little younger," he explained as, frowning, he flipped back the voluminous skirts to study the unlined interior.

I imagined a hefty teenager somewhere in Iowa, practicing her lines, nervously anticipating the rehearsal where she'd be asked to kiss the skinny cowboy playing her boyfriend. Oh god, what if she had to sit on his knee? Please, please god, let the boy playing Will Parker be faggy and theater loving, not some loud-mouthed, locker-room meanie! Make the dressing room a hallowed hall of compassion. Let not a fat joke cross the leading lady's rouged lips where the intended butt can hear it! Whatever it took to make my elephantine Ado Annie feel confident and pretty, I would do it. No one in *Oklahoma!* need know that her box social dress had been worn by a grown man with the measurements of a Frigidaire. With me as her fairy godmother, she'd feel like fucking Cinderella! "Maybe we could insert a panel somewhere," I ventured.

Steven patted me on the shoulder. "Even for someone as good as Candelaria, that would be a day's work. Get a load of the yardage. It takes an hour just to hem these babies. Why don't you go pull the bonnet that goes with the purple? You're going to *love* it." He winked as he pointed me in the right direction. "Give her the parasol, too. Might as well go for the full effect."

Although I proudly considered myself a member of Chicago's theatrical underground, I had not forgotten the thrill of participating in high school musicals. An absolute dearth of singing talent had kept me in boring supporting roles, but that didn't stop me from getting off on the intoxicating scent of pancake makeup, blocking that occasionally placed me hand in hand with the opposite sex, and the charged atmosphere backstage. I had only to slit the sealing tape on my first return shipment to know that nothing had changed in the world of high school theatricals. The evil olfactory genie that exploded from that cardboard carton would have knocked Proust dead on the spot. Steven and Laverne lingered nearby, curious to see how I would respond to my latest assignment, which was to check each returned item off on a master list, making sure nothing was missing as I separated jewelry, millinery, shoes, and dry-clean-onlys from the things that we could wash in-house. "Ooh, petticoats," Steven observed with sympathy and a sort of sadistic relish. "There's nothing like the musk of Love's Baby Soft mixed with teen girl sweat." He wasn't just whistling Dixie. Tears sprang to my eyes as, gagging, I tugged the first offender free from the sodden tangle within. Deadweight with perspiration, it had been stewing in its own juices for several days in the back of a UPS truck. During the long journey, its wearer's perfume had mutated with the signature scent of every other petticoat-wearing, hormonal chorus girl. The odor was primal, yeasty, and horribly intimate.

"I'll get you some rubber gloves," Laverne said gently, looking as if she might cry herself.

"Ooh wee, what those white girls do in them petticoats to make 'em stink so nasty," Gladys the laundress barked, as she saw me toting the first load toward her Maytag. "Not too many now, baby. Don't want to go breaking the machine." She watched suspiciously from the ironing board as I added powdered detergent and selected a cycle.

"You really want to know what they do in their petticoats, Gladys?" Steven asked, idly twirling an enormous square buckle around his index finger.

"Don't you start with me, Steven," she threatened, brandishing her heavy steam iron. "You know Gladys don't want to hear no smut talk!"

"Look at who you're working for," Steven countered good-naturedly, always happy to get in a dig at the boss.

"Don't you say one word against Dick Kratt," Gladys commanded. "Not while there's breath in Gladys's body! And you put that leprechaun buckle back where it goes. Been sitting there since St. Patrick's Day!"

"I thought maybe it could hang out here until we need a pilgrim," Steven whispered seductively, as he slouched past her on his way back to storage.

"Ooh, that Steven is *bad*," Gladys giggled, as she applied the iron to a frilly cotton blouse with a lethal-sounding burst of steam. Of all my fellow employees, Gladys was the only one who seemed happy in her job. She was approaching seventy but never complained about the long hours spent on her feet. Occasionally she would take off her Ella Fitzgerald wig when the steam started getting to her, but otherwise she exhibited a Japanese factory worker's commitment to the workplace. She kept her equipment and supplies in shipshape condition, admonishing her slovenly colleagues with a hand-lettered sign tacked above her sink: WASH YOUR OWN DAMN COFFEE CUPS. GLADYS AIN'T YOUR MAMA. She coddled the malevolent Dick Kratt like he was her own infant, for which he repaid her by criticizing her somewhat less harshly than the rest of us. Physically, she could have crushed anyone in the joint. Years of wrangling sopping petticoats at an hourly wage lower than mine had seen to that. On the work floor, she was feisty and endearingly egocentric, but away from her Maytag, she was aloof, silently eating lunch with Candelaria, the modest, middle-aged seamstress who, outside of a few strategic sewing-related terms, spoke exclusively Spanish. I suspect the rigors of their jobs exhausted them. Candelaria banged out alterations and brand-new garments at a sweatshop pace, then went home and stitched wedding dresses to make ends meet.

I envied her. I couldn't sew for shit. My high school didn't offer Home Ec. Instead, a woman I baby-sat for talked me through the creation of a beige wraparound skirt with anemic purple flowers. My only related professional experience prior to Showstopper ended in disaster. On the strength of some wholly hypothetical renderings I'd done for Virgil's class back in college, I had talked my way into a gig creating twenty-eight costumes from scratch for a hip-hop Cinderella. "They've got to look gooooooood," the director told me as she handed me two hundred dollars, my entire budget. Well, they didn't. I knew it and, more importantly, the cast knew it. "Uh-uh," one of the evil stepsisters stonewalled, when I showed up with a granny cart full of Amvets purchases and a lopsided choir robe it had taken me three days to make. "I ain't putting that on."

"I thought you said they'd look goooooooood," the director hissed, as the female cast members glared belligerently from the stage.

"They will," I promised, feeling even more miserable than I had the time I tried to take my stepfather's precious Thunderbird out for a joyride, only to get it mired in mud up to its hubcaps three feet from the garage. "They're not done yet. I have some sequins I'm going to glue on. I just wanted to make sure they fit first."

With a withering glance, the evil stepsister made a show of trying on the wrinkled, side-zippered skirt I had slated for her to wear to the ball. The sort of thing I might have considered buying for half a second when I was on the prowl for temping drag, it was at least two sizes too small for Miss Stepsister, a good lesson in why one should always measure, rather than relying on the dress sizes supplied by the actors.

"It's okay," I gulped. "I can fix everything."

"You better," the director threatened, then informed me she'd added another character, a male page named Peanut Butter, who, it went without saying, had to look goooooooood.

For a day and a half, I tried to put the dismal situation to rights, but as the old saying goes, you can't shine shit. It gives me pleasure to report that the local press drew on the same sentiment in reviewing the show as a whole, though one reporter praised the costumes, which were credited to the director. Before the show was set to begin, I realized that I could never hope to deliver what I had promised, and I bailed, claiming that my stepbrother had been horribly mangled in a bicycle accident, which required my immediate presence in Indiana. Any twinges of guilt I felt dissipated when the director failed to express so much as a "how awful" or a "hope he gets better soon." To my credit, I did return the sewing machine she had loaned me . . . eventually.

If *Cinderella* taught me anything (besides that I had no business pawning myself off as a costume professional), it was that the presentation of the garment to the person who will be wearing it is crucial. No longer would I fish a wadded-up skirt from the tangled heap in my granny cart, releasing fumes of thrift-store despair. I observed how Steven and Laverne brought out the duds they had pulled from storage after measuring our walk-in rental customers. One would never guess Steven's true opinion from the way he handled these items, never letting a hem touch the carpeted floor, as appreciative as the curator of an exhibition of First Ladies' inaugural gowns. "Never give them more than three choices," he confided as we waited behind the counter for a client to emerge from the dressing room. "Otherwise, they'll never be satisfied. They'll keep sending you back to storage for something else, certain you're holding out on them." The curtains parted as a dough-faced dental hygienist took a few tentative steps in a fringed faux-buckskin dress and acrylic argyle socks. "Ooh, very nice," Steven assured her. "Very *Dances with Wolves.*" We rented a lot of Stands-with-a-Fists that season.

I was lucky. My first rental client was blind. She had been invited to a fundraiser with a Roaring Twenties theme, so I pulled a bright red flapper dress, with matching ostrich-plume headband and sequined garter. Steven lurked discreetly in the background in case I started to flail. When the blind woman came out of the dressing room, I complimented her lavishly and tossed in a pair of opera-length gloves at no additional charge. The transaction was completed without any major screw-ups, but as soon as she had stepped into the elevator, headed down to street level, Steven started to snicker. "You should have heard her pitch," he crowed to Laverne, jerking a thumb at me. "She told her she looked 'very elegant'!" Laverne doubled over the cutting table and howled, while I fiddled with a pincushion, pretending that I saw the humor in being exposed as an imbecile. Steven had a point. Of all the adjectives one might use to describe a flapper—whorish, irrepressible, drunk—elegant was not among them, particularly when the lady in question was sporting a nylon-fringed, frequently altered Dick Kratt original. Despite the ribbing I was subjected to for the next several months, I wasn't entirely sorry I'd said it.

It was a balancing act, stroking my customers' egos while steering clear of blunders that, like "elegant," were surefire bets for behind-the-scenes hilarity at my expense. Many times the incongruities of the rental department left me close to a loss for words. The hatchet-faced Maid Marians. Wives suiting up their duddy husbands in swashbuckling pirate finery. Chinless divas. Palsied dowagers in poodle skirts. I could handle these often-dispiriting contradictions when business was slow, because, unlike Steven, I would dive into storage as many times as it took to convince my customers that I had done a fairy godmother on them. It was a different story, though, when clients descended in droves, all clutching invitations to some charitable function that jettisoned black tie in favor of Ancient Egypt or French Revolution. These clambakes overtaxed our stock, because nobody interpreted this directive to mean, "Come as a peasant or a lowly drone toiling away on the Great Pyramids." No, it was Marie Antoinette and Cleopatra all the way, baby. Midway through my tenure at Showstopper Costumes, the same association that staged the annual Bar Show threw a giant masquerade ball that aimed to re-create the Old South amid the polyester tablecloths of the Hyatt. Several hundred lawyers swarmed the joint, gripped with Scarlett fever. The men were fairly low maintenance. The only thing they insisted upon was fighting on the Union side. Steven and Laverne started taking all the men when I proved incapable of remembering which side was blue and which gray. That left me the women, all of whom wanted to be Southern belles. They also wanted to look goooooood. I quickly ran through all of the boned gowns the gifted Candelaria had sewn for *La Traviata,* and as Old South Ball guests kept pouring in, pickings became increasingly tatty. The Cowbelles flew off the racks, accompanied by their bonnets and parasols as Steven and Laverne traded jokes about Hattie McDaniel lacing Vivien Leigh into her corset. I had everything under control until my first African American belle walked through the door. My brain just wasn't capable of wrapping itself around this paradox. Was it an act of historical defiance for her to sashay around in a hoop skirt, overlaying her Chicago accent with a thick Gawjuh drawl? Or should she have shown up at the Hyatt in a faded calico frock and head rag, sacrificing girlish dress lust in favor of a withering political statement? How far up its ass was the Bar Association's head to choose this racially irreconcilable theme, especially given our litigious society? I found myself wanting to call the Anti-Defamation League, much as I'd wanted to blow the whistle on Amoco during the Gulf War, but in the end, I bit my tongue and rustled up the best gown we had left, a bubblegum-pink satin number that Laverne had reserved for another customer. It took Gladys over an hour to press all of its rosette-trimmed flounces.

The other drag about the big charity events that sent customers to us en masse was that the entire staff was drafted to make alterations. Even Corky, the boy-toy receptionist, was a better seamstress than I. I broke needles left and right, hemmed petticoats directly onto my own sweater sleeves, and boogered up seams with great clots of thread that looked more like centipedes than the tidy ant columns Steven and Laverne knocked out with lightning speed. Everything about the science of tailoring eluded me, from placing the pins accurately to simple measuring. If a customer returned to pick up an altered costume, only to find that it was too tight, or too long, or that the seams burst when they lifted their arms, we all knew who had taken the measurements. I tried to make myself scarce when customers came for fittings, cowering behind *Destry Rides Again,* knowing that Candelaria, or maybe Gladys, was racing to right the mistakes I could not fix myself. While the customer raged out front, Dick Kratt raged in back, and the worst thing was, he was the type of leader who makes the entire platoon pay for the shortcomings of its weakest individuals. I was Private Pyle in *Full Metal Jacket,* except my coworkers never snuck up on me with buckshot-stuffed sweat socks to exact their revenge. Also, I never blew Dick away with my rifle, though I willingly admit to nursing such fantasies. It helped pass the time when I was styling wigs for *The Mikado,* a task almost as boring as currying deluxe Fluffers.

Why he didn't fire me, I can't imagine. I certainly gave him plenty of cause. As a college-educated, theater-minded dilettante, I felt increasingly affronted to be in a position where my lack of sewing know-how got more play than my knowledge of Chekhov and Shakespeare. Every screaming meltdown Dick pitched made me feel more militant. How dare he upbraid Corky for forgetting to call the company that supplied our novelty noses? Where did he get off shouting at Dennis, the delivery man, for sitting around the break room, chewing the fat with the rental stylists? Speaking of which, what right did he have to make fat jokes in front of Laverne? How come he got to pick the radio station? He would be punished! When my roommate's impoverished theater company was producing a script that called for several World War I doughboys in uniform, I surreptitiously carried off several Hefty bags full of the necessary articles, which to the best of my knowledge were never returned following their prolonged, free-of-charge rental.

Knowing that Dick rarely came in on weekends, I punched in on Saturdays with the sole intention of washing my own dirty laundry. If a white armistice blouse slipped off its hanger, I left it where it lay, stepping on it as if it was the garment's fault for not hauling its ass up off the storage-room floor. I went from owning zero seam rippers to owning three.

The only time I ever saw Dick happy was when he talked about his hobby, which was dressing up in the Butterfly Stripper costume he had designed for our *Gypsy* collection, while making no attempt to disguise his beard or bald head. Once he entered his act in a talent show at the Manhole, my old waiter pal Horse's favorite bar. For the entire week leading up to the big event, Dick ran me ragged, demanding that I add dozens of rhinestones to his majorette-style bathing suit and bidding me sit while he sashayed in front of the ironing board, croaking "You Gotta Have a Gimmick" in a nasal tenor. "Just hang on until Friday," Steven said. "His ladyship's taking the day off to rest up for his appearance." How serendipitous! My roommates and I were throwing a masquerade party of our own on Friday! I came into work but spent the entire day primping like a non-hip-hop Cinderella before deciding on the wedding dress from *Brigadoon*, a special favorite of Dick's. Like my stepfather's Thunderbird, it was not to leave the garage without its master's permission. I let everyone but Steven think that I was playing dress-up, a far lesser crime than stuffing the cream chiffon confection into my backpack, along with its veil. Although Steven was invited, he declined to attend, claiming an aversion to costumes.

Unlike the liberated doughboys, I knew the purloined bridal gown would be missed, so I smuggled it back on Monday inside a plain brown grocery sack. I had no trouble getting it past Dick, who was in his office with the door closed, screaming at the bookkeeper. The only problem was that the wrinkled-up thing reeked of beer, cigs, and armpit. It seemed too risky to hang it back up in storage, next to the kilts. Any idiot would be able to tell it had been rode hard and put away wet. Fortunately, the dry cleaner's delivery man had yet to show up. I shoved Miss Brigadoon into the bin, underneath a mountain of ridiculously ugly *My Fair Lady* costumes, even uglier than the ones in the Audrey Hepburn movie from which Dick had ripped off the designs. Shortly afterward, the delivery man arrived, and everything was hunky-dory until Wednesday, when he returned. I was trapped in front by the rental counter, pinning up the hem of yet another middle-aged Gaslight Girl. (That's an Old West–style prostitute for anyone unfamiliar with the terminology, our default choice for anyone who wanted to look slutty without baring her lumpy thighs.) By the time I made it back to the workroom, Mr. Kratt had discovered the aberration among the *My Fair Lady* returns and was haranguing everyone within earshot. His anger wasn't unwarranted. Dry cleaning was expensive—which is why I made sure my *Brigadoon* get-up was Showstopper Costumes' treat. Dick couldn't figure out why the hell anybody would be stupid enough to dry-clean a gown that hadn't been worn. Nobody had produced *Brigadoon* in over a year, and all three of his rental stylists knew better than to offer his crowning jewel to a walk-in would-be bride. Paranoia tinged with guilt seized me, and I began to worry that one of my colleagues would rat me out. Steven was the only one who knew about the party, but the others had seen me prancing around in front of the three-way mirror when I was supposed to be altering can-can skirts. (I did them later and fucked them up royally, I assure you.) To my relief and shame, they all kept mum. I half wished Dick would connect the dots and leave these good people out of it. The circumference of Laverne's thigh far exceeded the gown's waistline. Had Candelaria wanted to get tarted up as a bride, she could have gone home and sewed herself something better in a single evening. Gladys growled if anyone tried to drape so much as a lace collar around her neck, so disgusted by hands-on knowledge of others' hygiene that she refused to wear anything a stranger had worn before her. Corky the receptionist was slim and effeminate, but in a swishy pirate/Prince Charming/snake charmer sort of way. If it didn't look like it came from the pages of the International Male catalog, he wouldn't have been interested. Steven? He wouldn't have tried on a sweater vest if he knew it sprang from the imagination of Dick Kratt. That left me. Size 8, female, and blushing, with yet another seam ripper in my pocket.

shamey, shamey, shamey

They made us come in at eight o'clock on Saturday mornings. Oh god, I swear I didn't want to do it! Dialing numbers torn from the White Pages, knowing just how livid I'd be were *I* untimely ripped from *my* bedclothes on my day off for such a jackass reason. "If anyone from your organization ever calls this house this early again," one sleepyhead threatened, "I will rip your fucking head off."

The whole thing smacked of remarkably bad business sense, and I say that as someone who once thought she'd be able to make ends meet as a pep-squad leader for corporate picnics, cheering reluctant teams of junior execs and accounts-payable officers through sack races and marshmallow-eating contests. (I took myself off active duty after I accidentally crushed a pair of two-hundred-dollar sunglasses

I'd promised to look after while their owner ran about balancing a potato on a teaspoon.)

Perhaps *someone* who had been randomly selected from the phone book might have been interested in purchasing tickets to the International Theater Festival . . . if only news of this fabulous opportunity hadn't disturbed them in the middle of dinner, or bright and early on a weekend morning. But for the timing, the calls I was placing really could have been considered public-service announcements, a sort of fiber-optic Paul Revere's ride. There's nothing like missing out on an event because one learned of it too late. Had the shoe been on the other foot—and had the call come at teatime—I like to think I would have welcomed a friendly stranger's advance warning that theater companies from nine foreign countries would soon descend upon four local venues to present twelve scintillating shows in two weeks. Unfortunately, I myself had had plenty of notice regarding the impending festival, so much so that I'd been able to jump aboard what our coordinator, Regina, referred to from the get-go as the World's Number One Phone Sales Force.

Regina's premature accolades made it difficult to keep up the charade that I'd procured myself paying work in the theater. There was a resolute quality about her that rivaled that of some stage managers and costume designers I've known, but in the end, her background was in marketing. Having cut her teeth on aluminum siding and the Special Olympics, she spearheaded phone campaigns for various local museums in need of increased membership, the success of which had led to her current position. She told us she was thrilled. "Theater people are so *real* compared to these buttoned-up marketing types," she intimated in a bit of chicanery that caused many of the new recruits to nod eagerly, if wishfully.

For, looking around, I saw only one guy I'd peg as a "theater person," though he could also have been a musician or a fashion design student in his flowered Doc Martens, paisley chiffon pirate shirt, and mini-dreadlocked mohawk. The others all looked like, well, telemarketers, though I didn't discount the possibility that they were musical theater people. Whatever we were, despite such motivations as the promise of free International Theater Festival posters and tote bags in addition to commissions, the World's Number One Phone Sales Force seemed incapable of closing a deal. There was one exception. Regina had set up a large bell on the conference table with instructions to ring it "loud and proud" anytime we wrote up a sale. I suspected it was some sort of Pavlovian plot to gear up the slow starters, but with the mindset of the kindergartner who faked a bunny-eared bow to ensure her name would be first on the I CAN TIE MY SHOES chart (I'm not being hypothetical here), I anticipated grasping that sucker's handle before the first day was out. Alas, it was not to be. The first half-dozen times I heard that triumphal clanging, I whipped around to see who was outdoing me, but after a while I knew. Perry Wong. He couldn't keep his paws off the damn thing. How could that little slide-rule dweeb be having such success? He had braces, for god's sake, and one of those little plastic coin purse thingamabobs to hold his subway tokens. Who would buy theater tickets from *that?*

Maybe he gave good phone, better phone than me. "What kind of theater do you like best?" I'd challenge anyone who didn't hang up immediately.

"No kind."

"Ha ha. Maybe you should get out more."

"Excuse me?"

"All I mean is, we've got a lot of great shows to choose

from," I would stammer, struggling to regroup after unintentionally insulting the mark. "We've got puppets from France and this young Mexican company and this Australian circus that's supposed to be hilarious, like, *really funny.*"

"Yeah, um, that doesn't sound like the sort of thing I'd be—"

"Wait! There's a whole bunch more shows if those ones aren't up your thing." I'm not particularly gifted at speaking extemporaneously, especially when I get nervous. "Not up your alley, I mean. Tell me, did you read *Macbeth* in high school?"

There'd be a pause on the other end of the line, then a sigh, a sonic cue that the callee was too nice or too passive to wrest their time back from an increasingly pathetic telemarketer. "*Hamlet,* I think."

"Okay, well, there are two *Macbeth*s in the festival this year!" Dead silence. Shit, Regina was cruising around the floor, her head cocked as she "monitored some of the sales for quality control." "The Scottish play! You're really in for missing a treat if you don't—"

"Listen, I have some friends coming over for brunch."

"Right, I don't want to take up too much more of your time, but real quick, let me read you what it says in the brochure about this one company's production of *Macbeth,* okay? They're from Ireland and—hello? Are you still . . . ?"

Before I became one, I always envisioned telemarketers laboring in cubicles or crammed into a windowless room, but the two-year-old festival was headquartered in a lusciously appointed former factory loft. The executive director had furnished it with black leather sofas, framed art, and big bowlfuls of M&M's, which I helped myself to liberally, consuming hundreds of thousands of calories in an attempt to offset my lack of commissions. The telemarketers, excuse me, World's Number

One Phone Sales Force, rarely saw the rest of the festival staff. The ones who weren't off combing the globe for talent for the following year's festival adhered to a nine-to-five, Monday-to-Friday schedule, just like the people we were bothering nights and weekends. With our higher-ranking colleagues out of the picture, we were free to find the area most personally conducive to cold-calling strangers. "Not everyone does their best work sitting at a desk," Regina had said at our first meeting. "And come on, it's not like we're selling AstroTurf here. We can afford to get a little creative with it. Have some fun! If you're drawn to the window, sit at the window! If you need a twenty-foot extension, just tell me, 'Regina, I need a twenty-foot extension.' I'm here to enable you, not to give orders like, 'Sit here, do this, say that!' *You* have to find the environment best suited to *your* unique style, the one that's going to allow you to flourish."

That was all the encouragement I needed to stake my claim to one of the two tufted-leather couches in the executive director's private office. My fellow boho, Big Al, stretched out on its twin, his knees hooked over one armrest, his head propped on the other. It was kind of like being in a freshman dorm with a really cool roommate. He was a bad influence, of course, but that was half the fun. His penchant for gossip and goofing off was a lifesaver in a field where the built-in tedium of the work is distinguished by the certainty that every unanswered phone belongs to someone who, unlike you, is out doing something meaningful, profitable, or fun. Fifteen or twenty calls without once getting through to an actual human is par. Then there are the interminable, unlikely-to-result-in-a-commission monologues of elderly shut-ins who, despite their feebleness, are quite nimble at evading all attempts to disengage short of the unacceptably rude mid-sentence hang-up. Regina had devised a complicated system of symbols that she wanted us to use on our call records to denote busy signals, disconnected numbers, and answering machines. "Leaving a message on someone's machine will never, say it with me, *never* lead to a sale," she had warned us, a maxim Big Al consistently ignored. Whenever I caught him defiantly sneaking his verboten patter in after the beep, I crooked my index finger up and down at him, the way my mother used to do to me when I was naughty, but not spanking-naughty.

"What's that supposed to mean?" he asked, making the gesture back at me.

"Shamey, shamey, shamey," I chanted.

"You freak, *this* is shamey," he chaffed, whittling the length of his left index finger with his right. I giggled. Adherence to social convention can be quite charming in someone who's taken pains to look like a swingin' Carnaby Street pass-the-Dutchie Mohican. "Anyway, who cares? If I leave a message, I don't have to keep track of who I've talked to and who's not home and blah blah blah. Look, either they want theater tickets or they don't. If they do, they'll call back and ask for me. What's the big deal?" He yawned and stretched. "I'm going for a smoke. Do me a favor. If Vagina—" this was Al's rather uninspired code name for Regina—"comes around, tell her I had to throw up or something."

As the days went by, I found myself harboring a real grudge against Perry Wong, whose only crime was succeeding where the rest of us could not. I was incorrect when I'd guessed that outside of telemarketing, he was not involved in theater in any significant way. It soon became clear that Perry was a loyal audience member, an almost pathologically ardent supporter of what has long been described as a dying art form. On breaks, he'd chatter happily to anyone who'd listen about the hundreds of plays he'd attended in the course of his twenty-three years on the planet, who'd been in them, who'd directed them, what the sets had looked like, the quality of the sound design, how the Goodman production compared to one he'd seen earlier in a forty-seat storefront, now defunct. "I don't know how you actors do it," he'd told me once when, to my chagrin, we found ourselves waiting at the same stop for a bus that would not fucking come, an interval that Perry filled with his incessant, enthusiastic babbling. "I could never do what you do!" I found it quite easy to hate him. He was so unjaded and admiring.

"Why should he get all the good numbers?" I complained to Big Al as we sprawled head to head on our adjoining couches like pajama-clad coeds avoiding their homework.

"I know, it's so unfair," Al groused.

Actually, it wasn't. When the promotional swag she dangled to sweeten our commissions failed to produce the hoped-for spike in sales, Regina brought out the big guns, pledging that every time anyone moved a hundred dollars in tickets, he or she would be rewarded with a page from the Magic List. The Magic List was a computer printout of contact information for every person who'd attended the prior year's festival. It seemed all the more valuable for being a finite resource: Unlike the White Pages, the Magic List had the potential to run out, as Regina frequently reminded us while tearing off yet another sheet and handing it to Perry.

"Shut. Up," Big Al would groan, as Perry swung the bell with annoyingly undiminished zest. You'd think after a week or two, Perry would have knocked it off, realizing that with no real possibility of competition, the bell ceased to be "fun." Once he started dialing the Magic List, Perry pulled even farther ahead of the pack, piling up an embarrassment of riches in the incentive department. Regina, running out of ideas, started asking him to suggest his own rewards. Without fail, he would ask for another two tickets to the festival's most obscure offering, a G-rated tale about ice fishing performed entirely in Yakut. "Now I can take my whole family!" he cried happily when he had amassed thirty tickets.

"If I could get my hands on one page of that list, just one page . . ." Big Al muttered.

"I hear you," I said, staring dismally at the non-magic list I was slated to call that day, a whole page of Nguyens. Why should Perry the Enchanted Telemarketer be privy to all the golden contacts while the rest of us slogged through the phone book? The large, insular immigrant populations that made Chicago seem so vital compared to the white-bread community in which I'd been raised served only to further depress an untalented, monolingual telemarketer. Whenever I found myself staring down several columns of Garcias or Polaskis, I begged Regina to let me skip ahead, but her standard answer to this was that one should never make assumptions. Hooray! Not only was I a theater person who hated theater enthusiasts, I was a bigoted liberal! Shamey, shamey, shamey.

Frankly, the troops could have used some rallying. We'd already lost a full third of the Force, as people grew discouraged by puny, commission-free paychecks. The only thing that kept me hanging on was the promise of two free tickets to every event in the festival, a bonus for those who went the distance. What a kick it would be to casually ask grateful, penniless actor friends if they'd care to escort me to one of these world-class events. The power I'd wield! It would be like bringing candy to school. No way could I have afforded to buy seats outright, not even if I went back to Dave's Italian Kitchen. Despite the sales pitch, I wasn't convinced that any of these shows would translate to money well spent, but for nothing, I knew they'd be, uh, something. I couldn't walk away from the promise of those tickets, and yet I wasn't sure how much longer I could last without some Magic List action. I brought it up with Regina, explaining that some of us had been talking, and we all felt we'd do better if we all had access to the kinds of contacts Perry had been tapping with such success.

She looked at me coldly. "Perhaps if you and Al spent less time gossiping and more time on the phones, you wouldn't have to ask for a page of the Magic List."

"Yeah, but part of the reason Perry's doing so well is he's calling people who have a proven interest in the festival."

"That sounds like sour grapes to me," she countered as Perry sprang yet again for the bell, clanging it like Quasimodo swinging from the ropes on Easter Sunday. "He started out with the phone book, same as everybody else. Those pages are his reward for excellent salesmanship."

"I understand that, but maybe some of the others of us could pull ahead, too, if we were calling people who actually gave a—"

"I'll tell you what. I'll agree to think about it if you and Al show me that you're willing to invest some energy into the calls you're making now. Don't let someone off the hook just because they say they don't like theater or they don't have any money to spend on things like that right now. It's your job to convince them. Come on, you're a theater person! Use your creativity!"

"What if they don't speak English?"

"Ask if someone else in their household does. It's a fabulous opportunity, really. You know, it's a crime that we Americans don't speak languages the way Europeans do. Can you imagine what it would be like to see these plays without requiring headset translation? Between you and me, the sound quality on those things is not good. Not good at all."

"I'll be sure and tell them that."

Regina swatted me playfully on the arm. "Back to work, you."

Despite Perry's best efforts, sales were seriously lagging compared with the mid-drive projections. At the rate we were going, the festival's "finds" were going to "find" themselves playing to 20 percent of their venue's capacity, and that's if they were lucky. Only *Macbeth*, the British one, was holding its own. The executive director of the festival, a streamlined English woman with disturbingly mod spectacle frames, was brought in to give us a surprise pep talk. I felt intimidated in the presence of this dynamo, whose M&M's I'd been scarfing down so boldly in the off-hours. With a quick glance at her chunky platinum watch, she spoke of the telemarketing team as integral to the festival's success, the front line upon whom both she and the "ah-tists" were depending. I wondered if this meant we would be invited to the cast parties. "Now, I'm desperately sorry, but I'm afraid I have to dash if I'm to make my flight to Berlin." She rose from her folding chair, readjusting the hem of her tailored black pantsuit with a smart tug.

Regina scrambled to her feet, too, looking a bit wild eyed. "B. J., before you go, could you just say a few quick words about what we were talking about, about the lesser-known companies?"

With an irritated snap of the head, B. J. consulted her watch. "Right. The thing with these smaller companies, you see, is you've got to be creative because your average ticket buyer has never heard of them. *Jardin del Pulpo*, for example. Marvelous." She reached for her purse, a sort of upscale bowling bag cut from the same supple leather as her office couches. "The Yakuts. Their utter lack of sophistication. The first time I saw them perform, I felt like I was in the presence of these Stone Age beings. My god, just trying to fax their contracts! The nearest fax machine is a hundred miles away!"

"Uh, B. J.?" I asked, tentatively raising my hand. "I was thinking that maybe for something like *Jardin del Pulpo*, we could do some sort of outreach program?" She regarded me like a carnivorous insect through her severe specs. "Because I had to call all these people who maybe are sort of disenfranchised or don't speak English or whatever?" The attempt to recapture my sense of liberal self-worth was not going well. "What I mean is, there are a lot of Mexican families around Chicago, like in my neighborhood, for instance, and I was thinking that they'd probably be really into seeing an original play by a Mexican theater company, particularly since there doesn't seem to be a lot of interest in this show otherwise, but maybe the prices are a little out of their reach, I mean, if they wanted to take their whole family. Didn't the brochure say this is a good one to bring kids to?"

"Except for the nude scene, yes," B. J. confirmed.

"Oh. Oh, so maybe that's not . . . well, anyway, I was just thinking maybe we could make a block of free tickets available to the, uh, Mexican community . . . ."

"Quite an interesting approach to increasing revenue," B. J. observed. So much for the festival throwing open its elitist doors to the large family who ran the produce market at the end of my block. "Actually, we're researching the possibility of instituting a program such as you describe for next year's festival. For the moment, though, I'm afraid you'll have to concern yourself with those who can pay full tariff." She plucked a brochure from the heap on the conference table, flapping it as vigorously as someone trying to attract the bartender's attention in a crowded club. "Try and push the Yakuts. And now, deepest apologies, but I really must fly."

"You sound hoarse," Regina observed on Saturday morning, her brow puckering with what appeared to be concern. If she'd known me longer, she'd have realized that the Brenda Vaccaro huskiness only meant that eight hours earlier I'd been hamming it up in the late-night show, screeching my brains out when I should have been protecting my instrument, as they say. It had been a bad show. I was kind of embarrassed. Perry had been there, and although he was too polite to say so, I don't think he'd come away too impressed. Regina clapped a hand on my forehead. "Just promise me you'll take care of yourself. I'm short-staffed as it is. Jenny gave her notice, and Al W. called this morning to quit over the phone. Didn't even have the balls to tell me in person."

"Al W.? Really?" I croaked, raising my eyebrows at Big Al. I'd never exchanged more than two words with my taciturn, now-former colleague, but still, I was surprised. He'd seemed so committed—or maybe he was just odd, wearing his International Theater Festival T-shirt every day like a uniform. We called him Al W. because nobody wanted to emasculate him by calling him Little Al. It would have been appropriate, seeing as how he was noticeably short in the way my Al was startlingly tall, but you never know how standoffish coworkers are going to react to physically descriptive nicknames. Big Al had told me he'd be willing to switch to "Sexy Al" so that we could sidestep the height issue and simply refer to Al W. as "Fat-Butt Short-Legs Al."

"Don't get me started on Al W.," Regina huffed in response to my inquiry. "He bails out without warning and then has the nerve to ask me if he still gets his tickets! Can't give me one good reason why he's quitting, but he still gets to see the shows, right? Sorry, Mister, not if 'I just don't think I'm cut out for this kind of work' is the best you can do. Loser."

I could feel an idea taking shape. Maybe it had been there

all along, like an under-the-seat flotation device waiting for the yank of the pull-cord that would inflate it. I knew I should proceed with caution; what I had in mind would require finesse. I tried an exploratory cough.

"That sounds bad," Regina glared, still thinking about Al W., I wagered. "Listen, do you need to take the day off? Because I'd rather see you nip this thing in the bud than find out I'm screwed when you have to call in sick for a week."

"I'm fine," I demurred, reaching for my handset with the gentle resolve made famous by *Little Women*'s poor, doomed Beth. "Really."

"I'll take the day off," Big Al offered, lifting his head from the armrest.

"You! You're on thin ice as it is." Big Al and I smiled at each other as Regina stalked off to check on our coworkers in the loft's main area.

"This cold weather makes me sleepy," Big Al remarked, yawning. "Wake me up if you see Vagina heading back this way."

The next week I presented Regina with a two-hundred-dollar ticket order from my landlady, a hell of a good sport who made a habit of supporting the arts. She had even hired me to give her home permanents. "Didn't I tell you you had it in you?" the boss congratulated me, taking the order form from my hands and replacing it with the bell.

I wrapped my fingers around its clapper, lest it accidentally make noise in my possession. On those rare occasions when someone other than Perry had managed to eke out a sale, they'd all eschewed the bell, and I'd be damned if I'd be cornered into doing any differently. "I guess you were right, Regina."

"Oh my god, your voice!" Regina looked every bit as aghast

as I had hoped, which made it hard to conceal my pleasure. "You should be home in bed!"

Or onstage. Like any good Chekhovian character, I paused to remove a piece of lint from my sweater, concerning myself with the tiny human detail before facing up to the larger reality over which I had no control. "I'm not sick," I confessed. "I've . . . I've got this problem with nodes on my vocal cords. It's happened before." (Except it was my knee, and I was working in a restaurant, and I'm not sure they believed me, because the day after I claimed to have dislocated it one of the managers saw me and a bunch of my friends bouncing around in the Moon Jump at a street fair.)

"Well, are you going to be okay?"

"Yeah, it's just a pain is all," I assayed in the hideous gargle. As a child, I'd had a horrible fascination for the Little Mermaid, and how she'd wanted human legs so badly that she swapped her lovely voice for that of the hideous Sea Witch. The Little Mermaid died, turned into sea foam, whatever (lived happily ever after in the Disney version . . .), rather than explain her true identity to the handsome prince. She couldn't bear the thought of him hearing that terrible witch voice coming out of her mouth. Well, I had no such compunction as far as Regina was concerned. For good measure, I gripped my throat, my eyes squeezing shut against the agony of swallowing. So brave, braver even than my good friend in high school who had to miss prom because she came down with simultaneous cases of strep and mono. I was modeling my performance on her.

It was flawless. The only potential problem was Big Al. I hated deceiving him, but intuition told me that he was a liability. It was imperative that the mission remain covert in order to succeed. I felt like a CIA operative deceiving his wife.

"Don't be an asshole," he implored, when he saw me flopping down on the couch with my phone. "It's not worth it. You're an actor! Your voice is one of your greatest assets!" It's the nicest thing anyone ever said about my nose-powered Hoosier accent. "Just grab your bag and go. I'll tell Vagina you quit."

I flapped my hand to silence him, as if he was preventing me from closing a million-dollar deal. There was still hope. After all, my landlady's purchase had earned me two pages of the Magic List! The first two people weren't home. The next number had been disconnected. The fourth, fifth, and sixth had already filled out their order forms, which they'd sent in with checks the day after the brochures arrived in their mailboxes. The seventh was going to be out of town for the entire month of May. The eighth had passed away earlier that winter.

"Oh, I'm sorry, someone already called about this," said number nine, the last name on the first of my two pages. "What was his name? I have it written down here somewhere. Oh here, it is! Mr. Wong, Perry Wong."

"But that's impossible. You're supposed to be mine!"

"Maybe he was calling for my husband. We have different last names, and somehow we both wound up on your mailing list. Well, anyway, I'm sorry, but we already bought our festival passes from Mr. Wong. While I have you on the line, though, could I ask you to remove one of our names from the list? I hate knowing that the festival is wasting money on double postage."

Fuck this.

"Hey, Al?"

He lowered the file folder he'd been using as an eyeshade. "Yes?" he whispered, clutching his throat.

"I have a feeling this vocal-cord thing probably won't amount to much, but just in case I don't come back, there's something in my call records folder here that I'd like you to have."

"Is it bigger than a breadbox?"

"It could be."

"Are its initials M. L.?"

"Yes."

"Is it a . . . male . . . lover?"

"Yes, Big Al, that's exactly what it is. I heard you were going through a dry spell, so I went down to Boys Town and got you some action. He's in the folder."

"Aw, you're the best. Have a nice life, okay?"

I'd debated whether the coup de grace could be delivered over the phone and decided not, although I did allow myself the luxury of showing up a couple of hours late, figuring that sleep was the best medicine for someone in my situation. Regina received the news I was so regretful to have to deliver with unanticipated grace. "I've seen a doctor," I whispered sadly. "And he said if I don't put myself on total vocal bedrest, I risk losing my voice for good. I might have to have an operation, I guess, but how would I ever pay for that without health insurance . . ." —pause, grip throat, mono, prom—"Well, anyway, I should probably follow doctor's orders and shut up now, but I'm really hoping I'll be able to come back for the final two weeks."

"Oh, Ayun, I appreciate that, but you shouldn't push it where your health is concerned."

"No, Regina, I signed on for the duration." Like a starlet from the golden age of silent films, I compensated for the lack of sound by super-animating my lips and eyebrows.

"Listen, these vocal nodes don't sound like anything to fool around with, least of all for you, a theater person. I'm glad you're taking a doctor's advice."

"You're right, but"—grip, prom, mono, Beth, so brave, so brave—"Oh, I was so looking forward to seeing *Macbeth.*"

Regina, looking as if she'd just stumbled upon the Little Match Girl frozen in the snow, murmured something to the effect that she wouldn't dream of denying poor vocal-damaged me free access to the Bard.

"Oh, but I wanted to see them all," I whimpered. "*Jardin del Pulpo* and the Japanese *Macbeth* and the French puppets. Oh, and the Yakuts. Ever since B. J.'s description—"

"Please, stop talking. It makes my throat hurt to listen." I bit my lip and mouthed a profanity, to demonstrate just how darn frustrated I was to be letting her down. "Oh, Ayun. We know it's not your fault! Your tickets will be waiting for you at the box office, okay? Even if you can't come back to work." She pinched her fingers together, twisted them in front of my mouth, then threw the invisible key over her shoulder. Wow, maybe she was a theater person after all! A mime! "All right? Now, I want you to go home, get in bed, arrange for a friend to bring you some nice hot soup, and don't get up for anything. Not even the phone. Especially not the phone, you hear me? Let the machine get your calls. You hear me?"

"Loud and clear," I croaked, forgetting that my lips were supposed to be locked.

harlequintessence

My very first duty as Titus Galleries' newly hired receptionist was to report to the Four Seasons for an employee-appreciation brunch. The college friend who had suggested I apply at the gallery where he was making serious money was nowhere to be found, so I hung around the edges of other conversations, hoping I didn't look like too much of a dud. Meanwhile, a tiny woman with the vicious mug of an overindulged lap dog reeled off what I assumed were self-congratulatory sales figures to a couple of other middle-aged ladies in brightly colored business attire. A man with a marked resemblance to a teacher who had persecuted me in high school retold the entire plot of a sitcom that had aired the previous evening, pausing only to insult the manhood of a chubby Asian fellow who stood beside him, chuckling at the recalled antics.

I approached two young women who appeared close to my age, but they acted as if they couldn't wait to be rid of me so they could whisper about how weird I was. Goddamnit, where the hell was Grayson? I was starting to have freshman-mixer flashbacks. Salvation came in the form of a pasty-faced guy with whom I shared a halting exchange on the restorative effects of yoga. Temporarily suspending my bias against holier-than-thou, no-refined-sugar vegetarians, I stuck close as we were ushered into the dining room, reminding myself that I had misjudged the character of several of my close friends on the basis of our initial meetings. Also, I didn't want it to look like I didn't have anybody to sit with.

When the general *oohing* and *ahhing* that accompanied the muffin basket subsided, the lap dog clinked a spoon against her water glass. "I know I'm speaking for more than just myself," she rasped, "when I say we all owe a huge debt to Tomi and Bernadette Szkyskr not only for providing us with this delicious meal, but also for assembling such a fabulous, inspiring group of artists for us to present to our collectors."

"Hear, hear!" several of our party agreed. Following my new coworkers' lead, I toasted the incredibly tan older couple seated at the end of the table. "Vell, Phyllis, I tink ve should tank *you*," the man parried, stabbing the air with a jeweled pinkie. "Over 70K you not only wrote, but closed. No vone else even comes close dis month." He bared his lips, revealing a row of blindingly white Chiclets. "De rest of you should be more like Phyllis, I tink."

"Phyllis's client purchased an *exquisite* Grunkey," the woman to my right murmured, enveloping me in an overpowering cloud of gardenia scent. "And darn it, wouldn't you know that one of *my* regulars is an avid Grunkey collector. He told me, 'Gabrielle, I want to be the first to know whenever there's a possibility of acquiring an original.' Naturally, I phoned him about this new canvas, but he said he wouldn't be able to arrange financing until he sold some property in Barbados." I smiled sympathetically. "Oh, well, easy come, easy go," she chirped, as if remembering some Stepford mandate. "To Phyllis!"

"To Phyllis and a more profitable April," her leathery boss corrected.

"I'll drink to that," the sitcom man announced.

"*L'chaim,*" Phyllis answered, carefully encircling her stemware with pointed talons polished a rich shade of liver.

"So, what do you think?" Grayson inquired a few days later, unbuttoning his Armani suit jacket to lean casually against the break-cum-storage room's Xerox machine.

"What do I think of what?" I was on my hands and knees reorganizing the slicks. "Slicks" were postcard reproductions of Titus artwork, primarily of lithographs and other multiples, but also of scandalously expensive originals. Grayson and the other sales consultants mailed them to collectors and passed them out by the handful to walk-ins, hoping that some rube might be enticed to plunk down a spur-of-the-moment deposit on the real thing. Upper management had decided that the best way for me to acquaint myself with the sort of "art" Titus sold was to spend several afternoons tidying up the neglected metal shelving unit that housed the slicks while the consultants took up the slack at the reception desk. My hope that this task might unearth a postcard-sized antidote to the schlock on the gallery's gray-carpeted walls was snuffed immediately. While other galleries specialize in a particular medium or region—watercolors, say, or Japanese prints—Titus represented a diverse body of artists whose work was uniformly appalling. Igor Pouffet painted gaudy acrylics of slender ladies in large hats surrounded by shopping bags. Schlomo Disney's insistently cheerful, packed-to-capacity, faux-naif street scenes made me want to hurl. Grunkey's recurrent theme, as far as I could tell, concerned the pastel lovemaking of stringed instruments and pallid aliens with alarmingly elongated heads. Herb Gale's entire oeuvre could be summed up with one word: rainbow. The prolific Angus MacKraig made it possible for society matrons in Nantucket, Palm Springs, and Vail to see their living rooms rendered in lithograph and hanging in each other's guest bathrooms. Decorum prevents me from mentioning Amparo Ina-Alvaro's sad clowns. Pickett Pynchon I'll get to later. Of the three sculptors Titus represented, one specialized in heavy bronze casts of eagles perched on what looked like giant ashtrays. The others shared an artistic vision of basketball players and/or naked gymnasts emerging from chunks of Lucite. Coincidentally, both of their last names started with W, which made keeping their slicks separate a Sisyphean ordeal.

Grayson lounged against the countertop Xerox as if it were a mantel in a short story by Fitzgerald, but his tone was impatient. "What do you think of *this,*" he repeated, gesturing expansively. "Of the gallery, all of it, your job, the *aht.*" I squatted amongst the lint balls of an unvacuumed carpet, considering which of my answers might strike him as least laughable. You know how everybody has this one friend whose approval they doggedly seek, even though this friend's a colossal asshole who speaks in an upper-crust British accent despite having been born on Long Island? For several years, Grayson had been that friend.

"This one's okay, I guess," I said, reaching for a slick that showed a woman with Vidal Sassoon hair and a black cocktail dress peeling an orange. "It's sort of relaxing, the way the artist managed to capture those little glowing circles around the candle flames . . . and I like that bowl the oranges are in."

"Cahdozo," Grayson barked dismissively.

"Well, he's better than the rest of this shit," I was retorting as the swinging door to the gallery floor decked me. A sales consultant named Trixie flapped in, bringing with her an atmosphere of henhouse panic. "Where's the Polaroid?" she squawked, yanking open filing cabinet drawers and rummaging among the coffee filters. Grayson remained motionless, his lips pursed with wry amusement, as I made a show of helpfulness by rooting around under the counter. "It's not *there,*" Trixie cried in exasperation. "Why would the Polaroid be down with the cleaning supplies? Where *is* it? I have a walk-in who's all set to buy that new Pickett Pynchon, but he won't put a deposit down unless we can fax an image to his wife in El Paso!" She sent a stack of manila envelopes cascading to the floor. "He's leaving for the airport at 2:30," she wailed, clattering down the stairs that led to the shipping and framing departments.

Gerard, the consultant who resembled my mean former teacher, poked his head in the door. "Where's Trixie?" Grayson cocked his head toward the basement steps. Gerard chuckled to himself as he unwrapped a hard candy. "Well, when she surfaces," he instructed, "tell her that her rhinestone cowboy got tired of waiting. He just flew the coop."

"Didn't Phyllis put a hold on that Pynchon this morning?" Grayson inquired. A big believer in setting goals, he had nothing but respect for that coarse little cockapoo, whose stellar sales record he was endeavoring to surpass. When I had sought to entertain him by impersonating her brown-nosed toast at the Four Seasons, he had cut me short. "She's an incredible woman," he'd declared as I gaped in disbelief. "No other consultant—besides myself—can even come close. She doesn't need walk-ins. She conducts 90 percent of her business from home, over the phone." When I protested that he couldn't possibly be serious, Grayson had actually patted me on the head.

"Please," Gerard now said, giving his mustache a rakish tug as he confirmed that Trixie was running herself ragged on a fool's errand. "Phyllis had that sucker sold sight unseen weeks ago to that proctologist or whatever he is, her Pynchon nut. You know it, I know it, but try telling Trixie! Some schmuck who's in town for the National Idiot's Convention toddles in with 'Just Browsing' scrawled across his chest in neon, and she thinks she's landed the big one. Hey, how about a fresh pot of coffee?" he asked, waggling his bushy eyebrows at me before letting the door swing shut.

"Well, I cahn't hang around here all day," Grayson announced briskly, picking his way through the disorderly piles of toppled slicks. "I'll take some of that coffee when you get around to it."

The consultants drove me out of my gourd. I had been hired to answer the phone and greet whoever wandered in off Michigan Avenue, but they all saw me as the personal secretary-slash-assistant they all felt they deserved. Whereas the art gallery of my dreams boasted acres of negative space, half a dozen particleboard desks were crammed into Titus's front room, one per consultant. Only Grayson remained aloof, forgoing a desk in favor of carrying all of his paperwork in an accordion file. He contacted clients furtively, hunched over the extension in the small side room that contained Titus's paltry collection of Old Master etchings. Crowded into a horseshoe shape near the front door, the other consultants could not only eavesdrop on each other's deals, they were instantly aware if one of their competitors was trying to monopolize my time. When Gerard strong-armed me into addressing envelopes in what he fatuously referred to as "my superior feminine hand," Trixie cried foul. "Just because you give her those butterscotch candies, you think you're the only one who doesn't have to address his own clients' invitations to the MacKraig opening," she accused. "I need her to measure the Pouffets this afternoon!" Gerard winked, flipping me another butterscotch. "Gerard, this isn't funny!" She stamped her foot. "If I don't get those measurements to my client this afternoon, he's going to buy his niece a mink vest instead!" Midway through this tantrum, Monty sidled up, instructing me to type "Monty S. Chung" above the Titus Galleries logo on several hundred non-consultant-specific business cards. Raising his eyebrows halfway up his bald pate, Gerard wheeled to demand why Monty couldn't just write his name in ballpoint on the cards until his personalized reorder came in.

"The typed ones look more professional," Monty explained, as I struggled to position one of the tiny cards on the rollers of the reception desk's elderly Selectric.

"Maybe in Chinatown they do," Gerard chortled.

"What's that supposed to mean?" Monty demanded. Smiling mysteriously, Gerard stripped the cellophane from yet another butterscotch. "I've never lived in Chinatown, Gerard," Monty said petulantly. "I was born in a suburb of Seattle. I went to Ohio State, and I live in—"

"Yeah, yeah, Naperville, I know," his nemesis finished. "Hey Halliday, don't you think Monty looks like a panda bear when he gets all riled up?"

"One of you must have stolen the tape measure," Trixie complained, clawing through her desk drawers. "Because it's not where it's supposed to be at all."

Just then a gray-haired couple in matching designer Windbreakers stepped across the threshold. The sales staff froze. I invited the newcomers to make themselves at home, reassuring them that their bags from Bonwit's and Lord & Taylor would be safe up front with me. Trixie, Monty, and Gerard craned their necks, trying to steal a peek at the clipboard where I kept track of whose turn it was to attach themselves to a walk-in. "Gabrielle's up," I whispered. With a smile as ethereal as her face-lift would allow, the woman who had sat beside me at the Four Seasons rose from the desk adjacent to Trixie, leaving a vapor trail of gardenias as she wafted after her prey.

"No fair," Trixie hissed. "I haven't had anybody since that fatty with the fake Vuitton bag who couldn't even speak English! Are you positive this isn't my up? Check again!"

I fixed Trixie with a cold gaze, unmoved by her bellyaching. I'd gotten my fill of that shit early on in my restaurant days, when I was a green hostess in a brass-railed brunch spot. The waiters used to complain—rightly—that I ignored entire sections, slamming one of them with five simultaneous tables while the others rotted in hell.

Less than a month into my tenure, Tomi and Bernadette returned from an extended stay on their private Caribbean island and, without warning, fired their second in command, a loyal employee with college-bound twins. Shortly thereafter, I was informed that the brass required my presence in Tomi's private office. "Sh-should I bring a steno pad?" I stammered. No, I was told. No need for a steno pad. Shit, that sounded like a done deal to me. They were fixing to give me the whack, too. Why? Why not? Tomi proved himself capable of a tyrant's impetuousness when he nonchalantly announced that a ranking employee with fifteen years of service had been let go for no better reason than "lettink too many shoelaces go untied." My fingernails digging into my palms, I stared at the Lucite-ensnared basketball player resting in a nether corner of Tomi's massive antique desk. It would be a shame to burst into tears in front of the bigwigs. Although I'd been as good as fired when various restaurant managers had left me off the schedule for weeks on end and that pharmaceuticals company had called the temp agency to request that they send someone other than me, I'd never actually heard those two little words that make professional rejection so official, so final, so humiliating. I cringed before the coming blow all the more keenly because I felt like I'd been doing a more than competent job of smiling at the walk-ins and baby-sitting the consultants. At least I hadn't been lolling around on the floor eating chop suey for hours on end. None of the consultants had been summoned to this powwow, no one from the administrative staff or the basement, just Kathleen, who until the previous afternoon had been the second in command's second in command, Gordon, the assistant senior sales director (whatever the hell that means), the Szkyskrs, and me and my conspicuous lack of pantyhose. "Do you vant to bring up the issue ve discussed?" Tomi swiveled in his tufted-leather throne to face Kathleen.

Shit, why had I allowed myself to get so cavalier about my illegal xeroxing, running off hundreds of flyers for my theater company's midnight show in full view of Monty and Gerard? Actually, if anyone had sold me up the river, it was probably Grayson, in a bid to cozy up with the boss. Taking a deep breath, I forced myself to meet Kathleen's gaze, to refuse the blindfold if it were offered. Kathleen considered, fluffing back great gobs of artfully bleached hair. She was getting a bit Hillary Clintonesque in the calves, but her pink suit was still just a few sizes larger than Barbie's. Gerard had told me she and her husband kept four horses stabled on their property. "No, Tomi, I think she should hear it from you," Kathleen decided.

Great. They were going to put their paws on my tail and bat me around a little before one of them finally bit my head off.

Tomi gazed out the window, frowning. Buckley, the pony-tailed office manager, hurried past on the other side of the glass, carrying a stack of computer printouts and wearing a constipated expression. It seemed only yesterday that I had been leeching him for conversation-extending observations about yoga. Now I was a bona fide member of the team. Gerard fed me butterscotch and called me by my last name, Monty was going to give me a deal on his old Nikon, and the boys in shipping treated me like one of their own, but what did that matter to upper management? Tracking Buckley with his eyes, Tomi asked abruptly, "Vhat happened vit Buckley and dat adjusted appraisal? I see I have seven messages here from Phyllis, telling me dat dis client of hers has still not received an updated statement."

"Is this for Dr. Rose? If it's for Dr. Rose, those appraisals went out. Of course, I'll double-check, but that's really Phyllis's responsibility," Kathleen gabbled.

"Who does a girl have to blow around here to get her pink slip?" I cried in exasperation. No, just kidding. In reality, I sat there meek as a lamb, willing myself not to cry when the final blow was struck.

"I don't see why Phyllis feels the need to involve Tomi in whether or not she failed to supply Dr. Rose's appraisals," Gordon complained. I wasn't exactly sure how Gordon fit into the scheme of things; I just knew that his underlings were fond of mocking him whenever his back was turned. He lorded it over the sales consultants but toadied up to the Szkyskrs and Kathleen. His convoluted title was no help. As best I could figure out, he was sort of the second, second, second in command. He had the grandiose manners of some lawyers I had baby-sat for in high school, but to reach the toilet, you had to pass through his private office. It rankled him. I was amazed when he revealed that he was only two years older than I was. He had a frumpy wife and two pudgy little girls and a house in the suburbs and the beginnings of a comb-over, all of which conspired to make me feel incredibly bohemian.

"That's exactly right, Gordon," Kathleen exclaimed. "It's up to Phyllis to keep her clients appraised, and if she's having a problem, she shouldn't bother Tomi, she should come to you or me or have Buckley check the figures on the master list."

"The real question here," Tomi insisted, "Is vhy Dr. Rose needs to fight for his updated appraisals. If Phyllis had been sending dem regularly . . ."

Their lack of consideration was outrageous. I'd like to think that if I had horses and a Corvette and a Caribbean island and enough money to wallpaper an entire housing project with raw silk, I wouldn't keep some poor little six-dollar-an-hour receptionist waiting for me to fire her. There was a chance I'd be able to make a matinee at the Water Tower, if they could only bring themselves to stop their eternal shilly-shallying.

"If you're talking about seven Pickett Pynchons, I typed up the updated appraisals and mailed them out Tuesday," I interrupted.

"Are you absolutely certain?" Gordon demanded, as if he was secretly hoping I wasn't. "Dr. Rose is one of our most valued collectors. It's imperative that he have the most recent figures."

"Yeah. Pickett Pynchon, right? That one with the clown and six others."

"*Ataraxia?*" Gordon asked, breathlessly.

"The one with the clown selling balloons in front of the Board of Trade. I can't remember its title. It was something like that. Some . . . word."

"There is a god," Gordon announced dramatically.

Kathleen turned to Tomi with an impish smile. "Didn't I tell you she was good?"

"Katleen here seems to tink you have a head for our sort of business," Tomi said, appraising me with eyes that looked like ball bearings buried deep in leather pouches.

"She's a goddess," Kathleen cried. Say *what?*

"Ve'll see," Tomi shrugged. "Vrom now on, you vork for Katleen. No more phones."

"I've been promoted to gallery manager," Kathleen informed me, smiling warmly. "Gordon is moving over to assistant gallery manager, and, should you choose to accept, you'll be my assistant. You'll help with every aspect of running the gallery: contacting vendors, overseeing any limited-edition prints that we publish, serving as a liaison between the consultants, and . . ."

"You can talk about dis somevhere else," Tomi announced, flapping his hand toward the door. Everyone jumped to their feet.

"Of course, we're prepared to offer you a slight raise," Kathleen smiled as she gathered up several pounds of paperwork, her Waterford pen, and her quilted Chanel bag. Who the hell was this woman and, more importantly, who did she think I was? "Goddess"? I could count on one hand the number of exchanges we'd had, most of them having to do with the Xerox machine's jammed paper tray. "We'll need to order you some business cards, I suppose."

Business cards? My thoracic cavity was suddenly awash with an intoxicating strawberry-flavored essence. I'd never had business cards before.

Tomi produced a menacing sound from deep in his throat, unfolding a pair of reading glasses as he reached for the phone. "Thank you," I remembered to say over my shoulder as we hurried to clear out. When Gordon swung the door open, Trixie stumbled across the threshold, leading with her ear.

So, metaphorically speaking, I was bumped upstairs, which actually allowed me to spend a lot more time in the basement with the framing department, otherwise known as Yuri P. and Yuri O. Not only did they keep their radio tuned to my favorite station, there was nowhere else for me to sit, since Tomi had ordered Gordon's former "office" to be returned to its original function as a broom closet. The tasks Kathleen assigned could be carried out anywhere, more or less, but I quickly realized that to remain in plain view of the consultants was to render myself a sitting duck. The receptionist who'd been hired to replace me was hobbled by her lengthy, airbrushed acrylic nail tips and some sort of mysterious malady that manifested itself in abdominal cramps whenever she was asked to do anything more than answer the phone. "Halliday, I need you to stop what you're doing and cover the front desk so Marva Lee can lie down in the break room," Gerard ordered, slipping me a butterscotch for old time's sake. "Monty has some invitations that you can address so you don't get bored." Kathleen bridled when she caught the consultants trying to horn in on my time, but I noticed that she betrayed me whenever the increasingly insufferable Gordon was involved. She really blew it with me when Gabrielle required help to close a lucrative deal with a waffling European couple. As they were going into seclusion in Tomi's office, Gordon announced that I would baby-sit the couple's little girl in the gallery while he and Kathleen helped Gabrielle point out the subtler qualities in Herb Gale's rainbow-saturated seascapes. I expected Kathleen to snap that I had plenty of more important matters to attend to—but not a peep. Before I knew it, the only thing between my lap and a reeking disposable diaper was a pair of size-2 rumba tights worn by an indifferent Italian toddler whose mucus-clotted nostrils failed to charm. With no toys to entertain the child, I hoisted her up to look at the happy shoppers, hot dog vendors, and street mimes populating the Schlomo Disneys. "Look at how ugly these are," I cooed. "What kind of idiot spends good money on shit like this? Not *bella* at all, *sì?*" After forty-five interminable minutes, her parents finally emerged from Tomi's office saying that they needed to think about it a little longer before they could commit to a sale.

"Oh, here's that little sweetheart," Kathleen enthused, avoiding my eye as I unloaded my stinking charge. "Gordon, how did you know that Ayun would be so utterly wonderful with children? She's simply a goddess!"

The consultants were all abuzz with the news that Titus Galleries was about to publish Pickett Pynchon's first poster. Even a weak seller like Trixie stood to rack up some figures, since this "extremely special" limited edition (of five thousand) was priced to move. This was possible because, unlike Pynchon's lithos, which were hand-pulled on expensive stock, this baby was machine-slapped onto the same flimsy, Spencer's Gifts shit one finds on dorm-room walls. I got a sneak preview of the extreme specialness when the Kyoto-based printers who'd printed all of Pynchon's prior multiples lost everything in a typhoon before they could begin work on the poster. With Atelier Sakamoto out of commission for at least a year, Kathleen awarded the job to a local printer, which is how I came to find myself way the fuck west on Belmont, rubbing my eyes and, alternately, my back as several ink-stained Teamster-wannabes referred to me not so discreetly as a cunt. But I get ahead of myself. Kathleen's faith in my abilities was such that when the new printer called to say the posters were done, she sent me to inspect the workmanship, telling me to pull several examples at random from the stack of five thousand before bestowing Titus Galleries' official approval. The first two I looked at were fine, but the third had a slight half-moon-shaped dent off to the right. If the dent had been two inches to the left, it probably would have been unnoticeable, lost amid the plumage of a peacock's tail, but mired in the metallic gray background upon which Pynchon's image floated, it counted as serious damage. I laid the wounded poster to the side and pulled another from the stack. Same thing. And another. And another. I called HQ and had Marva Lee patch me through to the boss. "Uh, Kathleen, I think there may be a problem with *Harlequintessence.* It looks like the whole stack of them has been laid on top of a pea or something."

"Oh, you've got to be kidding. Well, you'll just have to go through and check them individually."

"Me? But don't you want to take a look?" No, she preferred to trust her goddess's judgment. I dropped my voice to a whisper. "Listen, the main guy here insists this is no big deal."

"Of course not! He doesn't want to take responsibility for mishandling the prints!"

Ten thousand mimes embracing behind five thousand peacocks as five thousand full moons illuminated the ripples on the Lincoln Park lagoon. I could have cried. Two eyeballs multiplied by five fucking thousand *Harlequintessences* and divided by four thousand three hundred and twenty-seven fingernail-shaped dents. You do the math.

The smell of ink puts me on edge to this day. I associate it with being called a twat. When I got married, I xeroxed our wedding invitations myself, just in case.

While my friends west on Belmont were redoing the entire

job, gratis, I was preparing for *Harlequintessence's* gala opening reception. Making a black-velvet-draped folding table covered in crudités from Jewel-Osco look elegant was work, especially for someone whose natural affinities lay solidly in the hippie camp. Because I enjoy entertaining almost as much as I enjoy absconding with cheap wine nicked from work, planning my first few opening receptions had seemed like nerve-wracking fun, but by now the novelty had worn off. Also, even though the print shop staff's shoddy workmanship was directly responsible for the hours I had spent individually assessing five thousand posters for minor dents, I preferred to blame the artist. I'd never met him, but I was more than happy to think of him as a real dick. The bio accompanying slicks of his work described Pickett Pynchon as an Englishman who'd fallen in love with the vibrancy of Chicago and the verdant loveliness of its surrounding suburbs. (I hasten to add that I had nothing to do with the wording of that bio.) Even without the five thousand peacocks imprinted on my retinas and the distasteful experience of being called a cunt when I was merely carrying out orders, there were several compelling reasons to regard Pynchon with even more hostility than Titus's other sucky artists. First, Gordon idolized him, and I swore to God, if Gordon used his proximity to Kathleen to send me on one more goddamn errand, I was going to surreptitiously scrawl "Gordon is a big, fatuous baby" on one of Schlomo Disney's street scenes. Pynchon's grandiose titles also stuck in my craw, even if they did provide hours of playtime fun when Yuri O. and I got to lobbing alternate suggestions back and forth in the basement. Our fake titles were so juvenile that none of them bear repeating. Okay, "Jockstrapivariousness," but that's all you're getting. Pynchon's bio, if true, was the greatest affront, since I too had fallen in love with the vibrancy of Chicago—if not its surrounding suburbs. How dare he misrepresent our beloved city as a series of dull tourist attractions gunked up with a bunch of Renaissance Faire imagery? Where were the un-air-conditioned black box theaters, the burning trash cans of Maxwell Street, the dingy West Side luncheonette named after its octogenarian proprietress who still presided over the grill, running her hands through young male customers' hair and referring to bacon as "salt pork"? I should have challenged him to a duel.

Instead, I was staggered to discover how inoffensive I found him when, two days before the opening, he was ushered downstairs to sign the new, undented batch of *Harlequintessence,* all five thousand of them. He was completely passive, a wan, good-natured presence with the teeth of an elderly horse and breath like an open sewer. I didn't hold it against the artist that Grayson, by virtue of his fraudulent British accent, was invited down to share cup after cup of the black coffee Kathleen or Gordon bade me—me, the dent-catcher—fetch. I didn't fob my displeasure off on him when his wife/manager, in the throes of something she gaily called a "nickey fit," asked if "the girl" could be dispatched to procure more "ciggies." I honed his pencils in the Yuris' sharpener without complaint. When the Pynchons left, he called me Amy, as in, "Will we be seeing you at the opening, Amy?" He was making a courteous attempt to include the lowly errand girl. Apparently, no one had informed him that I was the mastermind behind all the little niceties of Titus's artists' receptions, continually exceeding expectations by schlepping my grandmother's sterling tea trays on the bus or improvising a cutting board for lemons and limes on the flap of the copying machine. I emptied the butt-filled mugs Pynchon and his wife had deposited throughout the basement, wondering at the miraculous transformation in my attitude toward the perpetrator of such art crimes as "Unicornicopious," "Demi-moderne," and "Scherezadium." When you got past the helium balloons and swans littering his canvases and the laughably overripe titles, he was just another decent-enough guy making bad art. True, he was one of those lucky few who didn't require a day job to stay afloat, but he had bad teeth and worse breath and a bunch of minions who stood to profit from him. Clearly, they were the ones to resent.

Meeting Pickett Pynchon was one of those Joseph Campbell experiences—from that point on, my gallery life started to unravel. Someone reported to Kathleen that I had been making sport of her relationship with Gordon, and she called me into her office to say that she was shocked—shocked!—that I would do such a thing. She was a married woman. Had I not seen the roses her husband had sent on their anniversary, with a florist's card thanking her for "nineteen wonderful years"? With the indignation of the guilty, I demanded that the sneak's identity be revealed. She refused, so I suspected everybody: Trixie, Yuri P., Grayson, Buckley from the office.

Then a small Rembrandt etching that was awaiting framing in the bin near my makeshift basement desk went missing.

Then Grayson didn't show up for work three days in a row.

Then Buckley's secretary, Shaneequa, was fired. Shaneequa had nothing to do with the theft of *The Small Jewish Bride,* but it was a bummer because she had a side business dealing weed.

Then Grayson didn't show up for the fourth day in a row.

The Szkyskrs went back to their Caribbean island. While they were gone, Kathleen, her cheeks flushed to match her suit, announced that she would be leaving. So would Gordon. They were going to work for a big gallery in New York, and as soon as they could both obtain divorces, they would marry. On hearing the news, Gerard stuffed some bills in my hand and told me to order the biggest cake I could find for a going-away party. "Something pink," he said, his eyes suspiciously moist above his mustache. Monty took some pictures for posterity, and we all stood around chewing the Crisco-licious sheet cake I had dialed up. A tourist with big hair and turquoise-studded white cowboy booties broke up the gathering, as all the consultants save Gerard raced to attach themselves to her. "So, what does the goddess think?" Kathleen ventured as I started to clear her office of forks and frosting.

The goddess thinks Grayson stole the Rembrandt. The goddess thinks the art is for shit, and in a just world, the Yuris would out-earn the consultants. The goddess thinks she's hit the point where any work-related service she's asked to perform feels like an imposition. The goddess could always go back to waiting tables, right? The goddess thinks you shouldn't have reamed her a new cornhole for her impersonation of Gordon kissing your tiny pink high heels, not if you knew you were dumping your husband for him in a few days' time. The goddess suspects that with you out of the picture, she'll be heading for the gallows the day the Szkyskrs return from the Tropics, and great magic eight ball, if she isn't 100 percent prescient on this point.

nothing personal

Employees were supposed to use the bathroom in the back of the editorial department, where the art director parked his bike. The one up front, beside my desk, was reserved for members of the general public who came in to place classified ads. Everybody respected this rule except for the assistant arts editor, a pinched hipster in his early thirties dressed like a Florida retiree, circa 1968. It drove me bananas. "Felix, what if someone's here to place a personal and they need to go?"

"Not my problem. Let them think of that before they leave home. Hey, has the new issue come back from the printer yet? I need something to read in there."

And then he'd disappear for fifteen minutes or so. A quick whiz would have been acceptable, but every time Felix came slinking up from editorial in one of his Orlon bowling shirts, I knew I'd be inhaling sulfuric fumes for hours. When he finally departed, he left the door wide open as if he were proud of the stench he'd made, like it was a gift for me and the classified ad reps perched on high stools behind my reception desk.

"Felix Tatum, man," growled Clarissa, using a hand heavy with skull rings to bat the air after he'd laid a particularly offensive piece of pipe. Whereas her colleagues, Buck and James, spent a lot of time on the phone trying to persuade local holistic healers and clairvoyants to place ads to promote their businesses, Clarissa did nothing but manage the personals, some of which seemed distinctly . . . professional. The other free alternative weekly was considered superior to us in every respect save the personals. As the biggest freak magnet in town, our back pages made for juicy reading. It seemed that next to consensual play with fellow nonsmoking diaper fetishists, there was nothing the fringe lonely heart craved so much as a bargain: Our weekly ad rates greatly undercut the competition's. Our most popular category by far was "None of the Above," a catchall for folks whose sexual tastes transcended the norms of your average hetero or homo blind date. The none-of-the-abovesexuals never realized what an able fairy godmother they had in Clarissa, who excelled at coaxing silk purses from sows' ears, thirty-five words at a time. The ones who mailed their ad copy in with payment were out of luck, but credit card holders who preferred to phone in their copy often benefited from her on-the-spot editorial suggestions. One day Clarissa came slouching in from lunch, characteristically attired in a leopard-print micro-mini and Elsa-She-Wolf-of-the-SS boots laced to mid-thigh. "How was Greektown?" I asked.

"If you're referring to Dmitri, he's even nuttier than when we were together, which is to say *seriously* nutty. Food was great, though. He paid, thank god. Here, I brought you some flaming cheese." She tossed a grease-stained bag, mercifully pre-extinguished, onto the anatomy book I was studying for massage school. My old friend Lisa Hickey, with whom I'd schemed to start a backrub business back in college, had recently risen from the ranks of waitresses with theater degrees to become a self-employed massage therapist. Not only did she make money hand over fist, she got to burn scented candles in a cute little treatment room she had decorated herself. Determined to follow in her footsteps, I enrolled in the same massage school she'd attended, scheduling my classes around my hours at the paper. "Hey, Clarissa, you got some calls," I said, handing over a dozen or so pink slips. "You better call that guy Wally first. He says it's 'a emergency.'"

"Wallllllllly," she drawled, squinting fondly through vintage cat's-eye specs. "He's my double amputee. He's probably freaking out because he didn't get any responses to his last ad. Poor guy, he's a total sweetheart, but he's got this thing about sounding all macho. I keep telling him there are plenty of women who'd love to be with a guy like him . . . ."

"What kind of crack you been smoking?" James called, having eavesdropped on our conversation from the classifieds counter. "Dude got little bitty stumps for legs!"

"Grow up, James," Clarissa sniffed.

"Yo, Stumpy!" James squealed, high-fiving Buck.

"Virgin," Clarissa countered amiably, heading, as was proper, toward editorial to use the bathroom.

Naturally, I would have liked to have been a writer. Not only did they get bylines, but the perks were hard to beat: tickets, invitations to parties, and an Arabian night's worth of review copies, all of which came through me. Rather than checking the masthead to see if a particular journalist was still with us, most publicity representatives preferred to squander their clients' resources by carpet-bombing every name on their seldom-updated lists with free goodies. One of my duties was to open and sort the mail, pulling releases that had been addressed to the editor-in-chief and redirecting them to Listings—if not to the garbage can under my desk. People who couldn't be bothered to call to ask who was the most appropriate person to receive the information they were about to send went to great lengths to create attention-getting publicity packages. They got what they deserved. Any envelope caught rattling like a calabash was discarded unopened before it could dump tiny metallic hearts all over the carpet, a policy that met with complete approval from the higher-ups. A band known as Hell's Fallen Arches endeavored to lodge their noses in the heiner of any schmo who'd published a CD review with us in the last five years by tucking a foot-shaped lollipop into a four-page brief detailing an upcoming appearance. "Suckers," I thought, stripping the cellophane from the first of many feet-on-sticks I would consume that day.

Speaking of mail, the aforementioned Felix Tatum seemed possessed of supersonic ears as well as irritable bowels, for whenever I was slitting open the padded envelopes from the publicity departments of Sony, Simon & Schuster, and the like, he'd appear, licking his chops like a housecat. The editor-in-chief had issued repeated edicts concerning distribution of review copies. As soon as I'd pulled them from their envelopes, I was to put them in a bin and carry them straight back to his office. The writers knew they were to keep their dirty little paws off them until he'd had a chance to overlook the latest plunder personally. The man's CD collection could have sunk a battleship. "Felix," I'd beg, "put that book back. Do you want to get me in trouble with Kane?"

"Kane can blow me," he muttered, pushing his porkpie hat higher up his skull as he studied the back cover of a soon-to-be-published underground comics anthology. "Besides, you've got three copies right there." Did he think I couldn't count? Three meant one for Kane, plus a buffer copy to distract from the one I planned to stuff in my bag when the classified ad reps turned their backs. Felix moved my coffee cup to rest a skinny haunch on one corner of my desk. "Los Brothers Hernandez, *cool*," he decreed, ticking off the contributors to the anthology for my benefit. "Chris Ware, that's a no-brainer. Peter Bagge, his earlier stuff rocked. Oh yeah, her. She sucks, but I guess they feel obligated to include a woman in there somewhere. Whoa! Tony Shapinus, no way! I didn't think anybody but me had ever heard of him!"

"I know Tony Shapinus," I whispered, gripping the edge of my desk to keep from scratching deep furrows into his self-congratulatory mug.

"You do? God, that's weird. I know plenty of comix geeks, but I've never met anyone else who . . . how come *you* know about Tony Shapinus? You don't read *Titty Twister*, do you?"

"He's my friend's brother." I held out my hand for the anthology. Felix paid my upturned palm no heed, but his expression thawed so totally, I grew alarmed that he might try to give me a hug.

"Holy dogshit, have you met him? That's insane!" I've since learned that every reporter covering the arts has an Achilles heel, some character actor or obscure painter the mere mention of whom will reduce the writer's cool pose to a jiggly aspic of pop fanaticism. "You know Tony Shapinus! Trust me, you have no idea how cool that is!"

I'm not sure who read our paper. Everyone I knew preferred the competition, except for one friend who said that one of the comic strips we ran was so lame, he had become obsessed with it. The circulation department, otherwise known as Mikey, would probably have considered him a "regular" reader. More typical was the irate call I once answered from someone who'd given a homeless guy on the subway a dollar in exchange for our free newspaper. "I thought it was that *Street Smart* rag that benefits the homeless!" the caller barked. I thought maybe he wanted to report the incident before others could be similarly hoodwinked, but no, he wanted us to refund his money. "Do people actually read this thing?" he'd sputtered.

"Well, *I* read it," I told him. I really did, when the phones were slow or Clarissa was too busy to chat or I wearied of trying to memorize human anatomy for massage school using a moth-eaten theater major's brain. Although most of the writers tried to behave as if it was all birdcage lining to them, I knew that they pored over their own work, bemoaning beloved sentences butchered by the editor's red pen, savoring the handful that made it into the paper unscathed. Felix Tatum talked about his stories as if they had been written by someone on the order of Hemingway or Tony Shapinus. "Did you read it yet?" he'd demand, and I'd shake my head, even though more often than not, I had. His beat appealed to me much more than the other writers' long-winded investigations into local recycling ordinances or skateboarding controversies. Anyone associated with a small-potatoes arts group, such as the one to which I belonged, checked the listings and capsule reviews obsessively, praying that their projects had gotten some ink.

I think it's also semi-safe to say that Wally the double amputee read the paper . . . or at least part of it.

If I'm remembering my Garfield correctly, receptionists hate Mondays, but I found Wednesday to be the cruelest day of the week. The paper went to bed on Tuesday afternoon and was supposed to hit the streets by Wednesday evening at the very latest, but this seldom came off without a hitch. There was always some crisis involving the printer or the delivery drivers, and by 11 AM every Wednesday, the circulation manager's natural rock 'n' roll petulance had boiled over into a full-scale diva fit. Nothing I could say would convince him to accept a phone call from someone seeking his guidance on a matter of critical urgency. "I'm not interested in hearing any more of that fuckhead's lame excuses," he'd shout, tossing his mane. "Either he does the job he was hired to do or he takes a fucking hike! His choice!" I've always had trouble mustering sympathy for people who are good at lavishing it upon themselves, but I did feel for the drivers, most of whom seemed too hapless to lie convincingly. There was one dude who claimed his carburetor was busted every time it snowed. He could have learned a trick or two from my old boyfriend Nate, who never hesitated to phone the manager of whatever restaurant he happened to be working in to explain that he couldn't show up for his shift because he had explosive diarrhea. He claimed that he'd never had a superior question the veracity of this statement, and, heaven knows, Nate went through jobs like chocolate-covered cherries—which is why he was able to use the dead-grandmother excuse fifteen times.

To complicate matters further, Wednesdays were the days Kane, the editor-in-chief, handed me the latest issues of *Publishers Weekly*, *Billboard*, and half a dozen other industry-related trades through which he'd gone with a red marker, liberally circling new titles for which he wanted review copies. This drove me absolutely barking mad. I told myself that if I ever got to be a big cheese, I wouldn't just go through the trades with a red Sharpie, circling as indiscriminately as a rampaging Hun. No, I'd neatly copy the titles onto individual cover sheets, which

I'd then hand to my receptionist with the publishers' fax numbers penciled on the back for her convenience. In my current situation, I was entirely too dependent on a manila folder on which one of my predecessors had started listing publicity fax numbers she found herself dialing on a regular basis. By now, its corners were worn to the texture of mouse fur. All four of the folder's sides were covered with fax numbers jotted in a variety of hands and ink colors with no regard for the rules of alphabetization. Every time I had to hunt for Knopf among the largely irrelevant university and small-press numbers, I threatened to create an orderly card file of this information, but the transfer never took place. Truth is, a manila folder would be much easier to Xerox surreptitiously than a hundred index cards, and I harbored criminal dreams of one day bombarding these valuable contacts with review-copy requests from *Bongos et Berets*, a "new" magazine whose editor shared my tastes in music and literature and whose nonexistent editorial offices just happened to share my home address. Lotus-eater that I am, I never got around to designing the sham letterhead that such a large-scale con would require.

"If you are willing to open your devices / you will know that I sequence / the frequencies of the city!" The big man rocked on his heels, his nostrils flaring passionately, his eyes suggesting an instability that went beyond the bad beat poetry he'd been spewing ever since he walked through the door. If I'd found myself next to him on the subway, I would have switched seats, but as it was, I was trapped behind my desk. The classified reps were sequestered in Kane's office, brainstorming ways to entice small businesses to take out ads in an upcoming educational supplement. Most of the other staffers were out to lunch or on assignment, leaving me to deal with this unstable mountain of a man on my own. He brandished a drawing he had done on a spiral-bound sketchpad, an ugly if painstakingly rendered cityscape. "When I close my eyes, this is what they tell me," he confided, leaning in close enough for me to get a full-strength whiff of his T-shirt. Evidently, his eyes told him that the Hancock Building was a shade midway between Band-Aid and tangerine. Hopefully, that was as far as his delusions went. If the dog was telling him to kill brunettes with long hair, I was up a crick. He pushed the sketchpad a few inches from my nose, awaiting a reply.

"It's . . . lovely. I love the colors."

"Fifteen dollars."

"Oh, it's for sale? Gee, I wish I could. Tell you what, why don't you ask my boss to give me a raise so I can afford it." Resorting to this sort of fatuous levity was an admittedly pathetic attempt to get out of further financial discussion, but the crazy man refused to dignify it by taking the hint.

"We're talking about original art from a certified genius! Did you see what those art critics said about my work? Fifteen dollars is bargain-basement for a piece like this! Look at the little bitty windows on that building! Took me five hours to do!" In Indiana, his physique would have gotten him classified as a hill, and his mental processes would have earned him a direct ticket to the VA Hospital or the Wheeler Mission downtown. I was considering busting up that brainstorming session. One doesn't want to be an alarmist, but on the other hand, one may miss one's chance to push the intercom button if one waits until the switchblade is being waved around in a threatening manner. I decided the frosty approach represented my last, best chance at self-defense.

"Sir, if you're not here to place a classified ad, I'm going to have to ask you to leave," I announced, channeling every bun-headed cinematic spinster who's ever tried to prevent the hero from charging into the executive's private chambers. "This is a place of business. You can't sell your artwork here."

"You don't think I draw good?"

"I'm saying that this is a newspaper. There are people on deadline here, okay? They don't have time to look at merchandise that just wanders in off the street. Maybe you could make an appointment," I waffled. Jesus, shouldn't Felix Tatum be needing to take a dump right about now? I sure could have used some backup.

As luck would have it, just then the senior music critic emerged from editorial, coffee mug in hand. Noticing the tense standoff at the reception desk, he executed a near-perfect double take. "Yo, my main man! How're they hangin'?" Like many Americans, I felt that bespectacled geeks in boys'-department-sized madras shirts should refrain from bandying about stale hip-hop lingo, a conviction that was directly proportional to the paleness of the would-be homeboy's hide. Up until now, our critic had shown no signs of vocabularizing it Snoop Dogg–style, even though he'd made several press junkets to the annual South By Southwest music festival. After a moment, my massive visitor grunted a begrudging acknowledgment to the greeting. "What are you waiting around here for, bro?" the critic cried in mock dismay, circling around to the front of my desk without so much as a word to me. "You chillin'?" He patted the giant's slab-like upper arm. "Next time, just come straight back to my desk. You don't need an appointment or any of that whack shit." This from a guy who acted like I was trespassing when I brought urgent faxes to his cubicle.

"Bush wouldn't buy my drawing," the big man glowered, allowing himself to be led from the reception area. It was unclear whether he was referring to me as a bush, a bitch, a hairy triangle, possibly my own, or, most damningly, the former president.

The critic fired a reproachful look over his shoulder. "Don't pay her no mind, bro. What's she know?"

Nothing, apparently, as I learned later that day when the critic berated me for assuming the visitor was a homeless schizophrenic. Okay, he *was* a homeless schizophrenic, but he was also a darling of the outsider music scene who supplemented his advances from the record label by peddling original drawings. Jello Biafra of the Dead Kennedys had referred to him as "what the true spirit of punk is supposed to be all about . . . arguably the most honest and original artist in music today." What can I say? No one told me when I was hired that in addition to reordering office supplies, answering phones, and opening mail, I'd be expected to recognize greatness where it was least expected. I once put my hero, Art Spiegelman, on hold for five minutes, mistaking him for an aspiring nineteen-year-old cartoonist who compulsively rang up begging us to give his strip a shot. When I finally rescued Spiegelman from the hold-music hell to which I'd consigned him, he was far more gracious than the situation called for. I would have understood completely if *he* had called me a bush.

"Let me guess," I said to Clarissa as soon as the door closed behind a pockmarked woman in stretched-out stirrup pants whose hands shook so badly she kept dropping the wad of cash she'd brought to have her ad run for six weeks. "'Surrogate mother seeks infertile couple with no hope of reward.'"

"Nope. 'Rita Hayworth look-alike, 36-24-36, available for sophisticated evenings on the town or relaxing bodywork in your home 24/7. Outcalls only,'" she read.

"Oh god," I groaned, feeling bad for any Hayworth fans

who'd take that bait, and worse still for lovely Rita. Because of Felix Tatum, I'd had to decline her request to use our bathroom. She'd have to shoot up in the elevator, poor woman. Finally, the toilet flushed on the other side of the wall, then flushed again, and then again. Not a good sign. The door opened and out he strolled, nonchalant as a bachelor in his own home. Tucked under his arm was a review copy I'd been salivating over earlier that day, a fat volume of early *Krazy Kat* comics. "Have you ever taken a look at these?" he asked, stopping to show me the cover. "Clearly an early influence on Tony Shapinus, you know, the whole brick-throwing thing? Fucking genius."

"Felix," I reprimanded, "while you were in there, a woman came in to pay for her classified, and she needed to use the bathroom, but guess what? She couldn't because *you* were in there, again." I pursed my lips like Marian the Librarian.

"Oh, come on! If she'd really had to go that badly, she could have used the one back by my desk. Anyway, tell me if you want to borrow this *Krazy Kat* after I'm done with it. It's essential reading for the serious Shapinus fan." Grabbing his mail, as well as a few choice items from the boss's mail slot, he retired to the back.

"Can somebody tell me who the hell is Tony Scab Penis?" James demanded. "Am I supposed to know who that is?"

"Nobody knows who he is. He's the brother of a good friend of mine. He puts out these comic books, but they don't do very well."

"Then why, every time Felix Tatum comes by here to blast a dookie, he can't leave without saying something about Tony Scab Penis to you?"

"Shapinus."

"Whatever. Alls I know is, it never takes me that long to do a number two. If you ask me, whenever our boy Felix

Tatum's in there, he's yanking his wankie and dreaming about Tony Scab Penis!"

Kane paged me on the intercom: "I'm all out of that hand stuff," he growled. Another notable virtue of our paper, besides the freak factor of our personals, was that, unlike the competition's, it was printed on recycled newsprint—great news for our nation's trees, but not so good for anyone handling its pages. The ink smudged onto every surface it touched. I looked like a chimney sweep every week after I'd gone through the new issue, ripping out reviews to send to the publishers, a professional courtesy designed to keep them from writing us off as total freeloaders. The ink washed off skin with soap and water, but then you had to contend with the fact that the sink looked like someone had been grilling in it. Kane's wife had found that the least complicated solution to the recycled-newsprint dilemma was the orange-scented foam that grease monkeys use to dissolve motor oil without simultaneously dissolving human flesh.

"I swear to god, I just brought him a brand-new bottle of this junk on Wednesday. I think he must snort the stuff," I said to the classified reps as I went to pull more hand foam from the cleaning-supplies cabinet in the bathroom.

"Hold your breath," Clarissa called.

Reaching the foam meant climbing onto the toilet seat. When I was reorganizing the cleaning supplies as an eager-beav new hire, I had stashed that case on the highest shelf, never imagining it would be more in demand than the rolls of toilet paper and paper towels stored below it.

I was just about to hop down, bottle in hand, when I noticed an incongruous object on the bathroom floor. You know that strange feeling that comes over you when you come across a familiar item in the wrong location, like when your grandmother's china pattern shows up in a movie or you find a bottle of fingernail polish in the forest? I couldn't for the life of me figure out what a Hershey's Kiss would be doing, unwrapped, smack-dab in the middle of the white-tiled bathroom floor. Oh wait; unless Felix Tatum, in a reversal of the old adage, liked to eat where he shat. Maybe I'd have to conduct a little experiment the next time he was in the can: knock and see if his mouth sounded full when he called "just a minute." A minute, yeah, right! He could've eaten his entire lunch on the pot, given the amount of time he spent in there. That little Hershey's Kiss was probably just dessert. Leaving the bottle of hand foam on the side of the sink, I went in for a closer look. Okay, I'll admit it, I have a huge sweet tooth, and if I find a peanut M&M under a theater seat, odds are pretty good that I'm going to eat it, even though I know other people would consider it unsanitary. Given that there was no one around to scream "Ooh, gross!" a one-seater bathroom was actually a pretty serendipitous place to discover a rogue Hershey's Kiss. In fact, but for the toilet, it was exactly the sort of environment in which one would want one's chocolate processed—all clean, easily scrubbed surfaces and bright lights.

Except, of course, that it wasn't chocolate. Let me state, for the record, and for anyone with whom I've had mouth-to-mouth contact since, that I didn't eat that doodie—but man, talk about a close call.

To this day I wonder, did Felix Tatum really not know? Did it just roll out of his underwear as he hobbled forward, pants around his ankles, to double-check that the door was locked? I've entertained the idea that it could have been a nonverbal expression of *something;* what, I don't know. Hostility? Sexual attraction? Superior knowledge of the history of alternative comics?

"Do you think he squatted at the scene of the crime, or did he transfer it using an index card as a spatula?" Tony Shapinus's sister mused with relish. I had called her the second I got home from work to tell her just how close I'd come to eating the shit of her brother's biggest fan. I couldn't bring myself to mention the episode to Clarissa or any of my other pals on the staff. The whole thing just seemed much too personal to discuss with coworkers. On the other hand, perhaps a whistleblower was needed to give others the courage to come forward. For all I know, shitting in the center of the floor and leaving it is endemic, as much a part of the industry as classified ads and review copies for which no reviews will be published. Years before, when I was working in the *Chicago Sun-Times*'s customer service department, I shared an elevator for several floors with a writer whose fame cowed me into speechlessness. I had no idea what one should say to a newspaper legend, but now I do. If it ever happens again, so help me god, I'll break the silence and ask.

happy ending

A teacher once softened the grade she'd recorded on my report card with the comment, "I think Ayun's interest in theater will ultimately be of more use to her than seventh-grade science." At thirteen, I couldn't have agreed more, but as it turned out, intensive training in Greek tragedy led not to Broadway, but to a decade's postgraduate work in the arts of taking down phone messages, currying Easter bunny suits, and refilling Parmesan shakers. I sometimes wondered if a different major would have better prepared me for life as a gainfully employed adult—women's studies say, or perhaps art.

Then I neared thirty, the traditional age at which frustrated theater types—humiliated by years of unsuccessful auditions and the appearance of spider veins in their tired, table-waiting legs—decide to throw in the towel. It's okay to be stumbling around a suburban mall dressed as Bert when you're in your early twenties, conventional wisdom goes, but do you really want to be doing it when you're forty? Fifty? Shit, no! But neither did I want to relinquish my tattered childhood dream for a "real" job. I'd seen what real jobs looked like when I was temping. The college cronies with whom I'd once hung upside down on metal scaffolding, writhing menacingly in pour-foam-bedecked unitards (long story) were decamping left and right for "careers" in computer programming, mental health, local politics, and law. I just didn't have the stuffing for it. But then, just when I was succumbing to despair, Lisa Hickey came to my rescue. Good old ethereal, pink-zebra-striped-T-shirt-wearing, tofu-munching, fringed-shawls-draped-all-over-everything, spaced-out Lisa Hickey—of whom we other undergraduate theater majors used to ask each other, "How will she ever survive?"—graduated from the Chicago School of Massage Therapy's 600-hour certification program and started raking in the dough without having to compromise her slightly off-center dignity in the least. That's for me! said I, rushing to enroll.

And thus it turns out that seventh-grade science is, in large part, what has allowed me to continue pursuing my "interest in theater," as Miss Cooper referred to it, all those years ago. There were no frogs or periodic tables, but, at times, sitting there with my fellow students (mostly nurses, flight attendants, and corporate drones who overwhelmingly cited "soul deadening" as the reason behind their midlife career switches), the notes I found myself taking in massage-school anatomy lectures were so déjà vu I had to check that I wasn't wearing a uniform kilt. I loved revisiting all that stuff I had paid so little attention to on the first go-round—the names of the bones and muscles, organ function, ventricles, all that. Then we moved on to arthritis, fungal infections, and, most exciting for me, cadaver dissection! It was great! Finally, a day job that, like medicine, required rigorous study before it could be put into practice. Sure, there was a time when I studied acting as intently as my premed roommate studied, uh, whatever it was she was studying, but it wasn't really essential to my career—or lack thereof. Let's face it, there are plenty of naturally talented, completely untrained underwear models out there who are going to get the part, any part, over me, even though I know what *cathurni* are and they don't. But the information that gets imparted in massage school is essential. Without it, you could end up hurting one of your clients. You could fuck up a neck, you could dislodge a blood clot in a varicose vein and send it racing for the heart, you could fail to drape a gentleman's frank-and-beans securely . . . .

I was so rip-snortin' fired up to call myself a massage therapist that long before graduation, I got Clarissa to place a free classified ad in the newspaper for me, offering student-level bodywork at the bargain-basement price of twenty dollars an hour, a good forty bucks below the going rate. And I would venture to say that the thrifty pilgrims who climbed aboard the secondhand massage table I'd set up in my dining room got pretty much what they paid for. Everyone, that is, except for the eager fellow angling for a student-level hand job. Fortunately, the Chicago School of Massage Therapy, unlike the seriously deficient sex-education module that took place midway through my seventh-grade science class, equipped its students with a phrase for just this sort of occasion: "I'm sorry, but I cannot facilitate a sexual release for you." (I like to use it on my husband sometimes for fun.)

Hell, the stage has been set for misunderstandings ever since "massage parlor" became a widely recognized euphemism for sex for hire, but the grinders and I almost always managed to weed each other out on the phone. A caller who asked for a "happy ending" wasn't rooting for Richard Gere to marry Julia Roberts at the end of *Pretty Woman* any more than I was. At the height of my powers, I could heal a crick in a certain type of male caller's neck far more efficiently than one of those 900-number ministries whose operators offer up prayers for the sick at per-minute rates. All I had to do was give the afflicted advance notice that the appointment he was booking would be a "strictly nonsexual treatment." I reckoned that I must have made him feel better, because otherwise why would the line go dead? Explicit prescreening isn't entirely foolproof, though, so I always tried to present first-time clients with a professional image, as close to clinical as a former Moondancer staffer could manage. Anyone who couldn't tell the difference between "Sensuous Full Body Rubs To Be Performed By Our Gorgeous, English-Speaking Staff (24 hours a day, outcall only)" and what I had to offer—makeup-free in floppy pants, surrounded by medical charts featuring the flayed human musculoskeletal system—should have a) paid more attention in seventh-grade science and b) skipped ahead a few classifieds to the one placed by Domineeque 40DDD She-Male.

Soon my little dining room massage practice was really humming along. I'd amassed a healthy number of regular clients, and my upstairs neighbor had agreed to tone her screaming orgasms down a few pegs during my working hours. I'd just had my 600-hour certificate professionally framed as a graduation present to myself, when *bang!* my husband and I decided to shake things up by moving to New York City, where, I was shocked to learn, the licensing requirements were not only different than Chicago's, they were enforced! I wouldn't be able to practice massage legally until I'd studied a hundred hours of shiatsu and passed an exam. There was no way around it, but I was damned if I was going to support myself by temping or waitressing for the year and a half it would take to get that license. Instead I went underground, literally, by posting a homemade flyer advertising my services in the laundry room of my new apartment building. FREEDOM FROM STRESS it promised, in careful, purple-inked letters. Sadly, this attempt to drum up some under-the-radar business resulted in just one client—and lots of dark looks from neighbors who didn't seem too thrilled that a hooker had set up shop in 1B.

What had I done? How did New York State expect me to pay for this shiatsu shinola, let alone make rent on my twelve-hundred-dollar-a-month sublet, if they wouldn't let me practice massage? I had experience, training, and, according to at least three satisfied dining-room customers, "good energy." Surely, somewhere in New York City, some spa or health club would be willing to hire me under the table. I pounded the pavement, equipped with letters of recommendation and business cards with my Chicago number scratched out.

"Come back when you've got your license," they all said. I'd just about given up hope when, emerging from a bakery where I'd been attempting to drown my troubles in *ruggelah,* I noticed a second-story awning labeled SHRI DEVI TEMPLE OF HEALING AND ORGANIC SKINCARE. That sounded promising. I rang the doorbell, got buzzed up to the second floor, explained my situation, sweated through a twenty-minute audition on the owner's gluteus maximus (an unusual choice—usually prospective employers have you work on their backs), and, just like that, had myself a job. It was so exciting, just like one of those musicals where some gee-shucks nobody moves to the Big City and is transformed overnight into a Great Big Broadway Star.

Despite being on special terms with her heinie, I found the

boss more than a little intimidating. Terrifying, even. Shri Devi had spent forty years as Bertha Goldblatt; then, her children grown, her romance with skin care for skin care's sake gone stale, she divorced her husband and moved to New York from Israel to pursue her interest in the New Age. She was conversant in chakras, reflexology, Reiki, herbal remedies that she alleged could cure cancer (as long as the patient was "emotionally receptive"), ear candling, biofeedback, macrobiotics, and the *I Ching,* but none of these hippie-dippyish enthusiasms could mask her essentially bullying nature. It wasn't something that popped out when she was under duress. No, her capacity for wrath was a constant presence, rather like the odors from the chicken-processing plant adjoining the Chicago School of Massage Therapy. She was nothing like the blissed-out yoga lovelies shown submitting to facials and massages on her floridly worded brochures. Her body wasn't the only thing that reminded me of a tank. Anything that she perceived as an obstacle, she flattened, making sure that some scapegoat was held accountable for what was often an extremely minor *force majeure.* She drubbed the weak in public, bellowing scathing insults at delivery boys; tearful young receptionists; and a succession of nail technicians who came and went so quickly it seemed pointless to learn their names. She showed greater restraint with the customers, holding her eviscerating tongue until a wealthy matron had disappeared into the room, where organic beeswax and cooling floral essences would be applied to denude her of unwanted hair and more than a hundred dollars.

Then: "She's a bitch, this one. She complains to me that her husband no longer makes love to her. I tell her that she needs to meditate, then maybe he will want to fuck her again. But does she listen? Of course not. How can she listen when her aura is so terrible, brown like shit, like an unflushed toilet. It makes me want to throw up. You think I am kidding? Always, she says to me, 'Oh Shri Devi, you are the only one I want to work on me, not one of those girls you have, *you* . . .' Because, it is true, I have the hands of a healer. My energy is such that even in a waxing or a manicure, she will receive benefits. She begs me, 'Oh, I will pay extra, I will pay double, whatever it costs, I will pay for you to be the one who does my treatment.' But she is crazy, and she will never be satisfied. I tell her that she will get cancer if she does not do something about that aura of hers, but of course, she is not open enough to hear me. She does not deserve my energy."

I know all this energy talk can sound awfully ooky-spooky-whoo-whoo, but it's not entirely cracked. I've encountered it in the massage room from time to time. Since I don't experience it every time, when it happens, I tend to attribute it to some sort of mojo on the client's part. Some people just give off an incredibly positive, absolution-granting buzz that is best experienced physically. It's a kind of voodoo, this magnetism—in the theater, it's known as having "it." "It" isn't something you can acquire through training, practice, or surgery. You either have "it" or you don't. While I never received a treatment from Shri Devi, I did work for and on her ass, and methinks that someone who spends so much time bragging about how they have "it," can't possibly.

Of course, Shri Devi's unshakable confidence was what got me hired. Someone like her is not going to be cowed by the regulations of the New York State Education Department's Division of Professional Licensing Services. Once upon a time, a licensed massage therapist had worked for Shri Devi, but she had departed long ago, conveniently leaving behind a framed copy of that all-important document. "If anyone checks, you will say you are her," Shri Devi told me with a shrug the day she hired me, far less interested in the possibility of a licensing-board raid than in annihilating the receptionist for neatly folding a load of towels in some monstrously incorrect manner. Despite her confidence, I worried that this scam could bar me from ever obtaining my license, or worse, get me hauled away in cuffs for daring to impersonate one who'd paid her shiatsu dues the hard way.

"But this is ree-dick-leeus," sniffed Shri Devi's protégée, Minka the Polish facialist, when I confided my misgivings. "How they will check? Come on. For seven years, I work here. Always the masseuse is Katleen O'Keff."

"O'Keefe," I murmured, having committed my pseudonym to memory.

"Okay, O'Keff, this is the same thing," Minka cried in exasperation. "What you are afraid of? You are American! When I am coming here from Krakow, I know nothing except skin, okay? I cannot even speak three words of English! Oh god, you should have seen my hair," she giggled, her fingers fanning up from her brow to indicate recklessly moussed bangs. Then, hopping right back on message, she planted her fists on her hips and glared, "Without English, how I am to get license?" Minka had flourished under the table, squirreling away enough to purchase a three-bedroom house in Queens. At Shri Devi's urging, she had attended all sorts of weekend seminars on topics ranging from colonic cleansing to crystal meditation, but she'd never gotten around to procuring her aesthetician's license. I asked her if she ever worried about getting busted. "Please. If they are coming to check, I will say I am Polish cleaning lady." I wondered where this would leave the real cleaning lady, a ghostly ectomorph who came in twice a week to wipe down the blades of the ceiling fans and suffer the impossible-to-please mistress's lashing verbal abuse, helpfully translated into Polish by Minka.

Due to a turnover rate that would have been considered high for Jack In The Box, I was soon the ranking Kathleen O'Keefe, with a full complement of regulars inherited from my fed-up predecessors. I tried to follow Minka's advice not to take it personally when Shri Devi lit into me for some imaginary infraction, but in truth, I'd have flown the coop, too, if anyone else in New York City would have taken me on without a license. Maybe absence makes the heart grow fonder, but she seemed a thousand times worse than anyone under whose authority I'd labored, even the temperamental chef I'd had to deal with at Palucci's who once threatened me with a cleaver for saying a slice of cheesecake he'd slammed onto a plate looked too ugly to serve. He, at least, never muddied his diatribes with sick-making allusions to his own virtuous energy. I counted myself lucky if I happened to be sequestered in the massage room when Shri Devi's gale force winds struck, although we could hear her loud and clear through the fiberboard walls. For my client's sake, I always played it cool, both hands kneading away as if nothing was amiss while I used my toe to crank the volume on the bamboo flute tape Shri Devi insisted we play because it was so "Zen." Regular customers, knowing the deal, were unfazed by the proprietress's meltdowns, but new clients, spooked by the barely muffled, shockingly volatile insults provoked by a paper cup of coffee abandoned on the waiting-room bench, often panicked, re-clenching every muscle thus far released.

"*Shh, shh,* Shri Devi, this is nothing," I could hear Minka soothing. "It is the massage who forgot it, okay? She is new. She doesn't know. I will throw away."

"Americans are such pigs," the boss would growl, thundering past the treatment room's shoji screen doors to comfort herself with the secret stash of Snickers that lurked somewhere in the recesses of her "macrobiotic" pantry.

"Why don't you help yourself to a deep, cleansing breath?" I'd counsel, as the flesh tensed nearly to rigor mortis beneath my fingertips and I wondered if the overheard tantrum would have a negative impact on my tip. The best part of working at Shri Devi's was the miniature manila envelopes the receptionist presented to clients at the end, as they stood before her in their stocking feet, skin glowing and hair in disarray, fumbling for their wallets. I'd always hated having to come down off my high plateau to deal with money at the end of a treatment, back in the good old dining-room days. Now that I was a hired gun, I was free to hide behind the shoji screens, bundling up the soiled sheets while the receptionist did the dirty work. I especially liked it when she pointedly mentioned that gratuity was not included. Later, I could float out, pretending not to notice the tiny envelope with my name misspelled on it. "Don't forget to drink a lot of extra water today," I'd remind the client, now seated on the bench, struggling with his shoes. Eager as I was to lift that little manila flap, there was a pleasurable aspect to delaying gratification, something akin to facilitating a sexual release via the scenic route. "If you find yourself experiencing any pain back in that area between your shoulder blades, just slap an ice pack on it. Or if you've got a bag of frozen peas, those work great, too." Channeling Lisa Hickey, I smiled beatifically, a guileless fairy with hands of steel, my homespun advice sound but also calculated. I knew perfectly well the endearing effect it would have here, where small bundles of sage were priced at $14.95 a pop in a basket labeled NATIVE WISDOM. (Excuse me, Wounded White Back, I just channeled your totemic animal, and with regard to your question about how much you should tip, 25 percent should be about right. At least that's what Cougar told me.)

"I was really tight back there, huh?" the client would venture hopefully.

"Mmm-hmm!" I'd nod, wide-eyed, just barely resting my fingertips on an entirely average trapezius. Trust me, it's always advantageous to play along. His biggest problem may be repulsively unhygienic feet or the unfortunate dorsal skin condition that Minka referred to as "bacne," but anyone who's just dropped close to a hundred bucks on a sixty-minute massage doesn't want to hear about that. What he craves is confirmation that at least one of his muscles was supernaturally tight. It's almost as deep-seated as his need to be complimented on his ability to withstand pressure. "We were working really, really deep," I'd confide as, seemingly unconsciously, I gingerly massaged the flesh between my thumb and index finger, achy from the incredible jackhammering I'd been forced to perform when I realized the tortuous amount of pressure his zitty back could withstand. The devil is in the details, you know. I'm sure any prostitute worth her salt would say the same.

My twenty-buck classified offer back in Chicago had netted a clientele much like myself, but Shri Devi's exorbitant service fees, coupled with her prime location and glowing, if yellowed, clippings from *Vogue,* drew from an entirely different watering hole. I worked on opera singers from nearby Lincoln Center, mumbo jumbo–spouting devotees of the New Age whose Park Avenue apartments boasted bidets and private elevators, nervous heterosexual men cashing in gift certificates bought by well-meaning girlfriends, and supple-briefcased Wall Streeters. Not all of our regulars were wealthy. A handful were textbook Upper West Side eccentrics, elderly remnants of *la vie bohème* whose rent-controlled living situations allowed them to splash out on seaweed wraps, salt-glow scrubs, and me.

If only we could pick our clients the way we pick our

friends, I'd never have had to contend with Louisa, a garishly made up septuagenarian with a hunchback and a crumpled velveteen rose pinned in her skimpy black bun, who, like many underfunded New Yorkers, made a habit of agitating for all sorts of extras that weren't included in the price of the service she requested. Her lust for pillows, blankets, and bolsters was insatiable. At the end of every treatment, she could be counted on to remember that she'd forgotten to mention how much her neck had been bothering her, unspeakable pain, look, she could hardly turn her head, couldn't I spend just five extra minutes on her scrawny, ungrateful chicken neck? Back in Chicago, I had routinely exceeded time limits for clients I liked, but I didn't like Louisa. Her tips were as rent controlled as her apartment. Every time I caved in to the old bat, I cursed my stupidity, knowing what was in store for me should Shri Devi notice I had disrespected her authority by interpreting an hour as anything longer than the fifty-five minutes she said it was.

Horrible as she was, Louisa was nothing compared to the Ladies Who Lunch (in the kinds of restaurants that would never hire the likes of me). At least Louisa was a bohemian, and it's entirely possible one day I, too, might find that I am shriveled and nasty, with a dingy fabric flower clipped in my thinning hair, whining for pillows and blankets when what I really want is love (and five more minutes, free). But the Lunching Ladies, no. They were the backbone of Shri Devi's business and the bane of mine. As far as I could tell, all their auras were shit-brown. Following a "day of beauty"—consisting of a massage, a deluxe facial with enzyme peel, a spa lunch, and a hot paraffin mani and pedi—your typical Lady Who Lunches would ignore the mini manila envelopes, grandly laying a crisp fiver on the counter with instructions for the receptionist to split it up among "the girls." I had half a mind to avenge myself by revealing that their "spa" lunches came from the pay-by-the-pound salad bar at the Korean corner deli, the one that had been featured prominently in a New York 1 *HealthWatch* exposé. Fortunately, the other half of my mind, the half that reluctantly prizes self-preservation above payback, always prevailed. It's no stretch to imagine Shri Devi smashing my orthodontia with a bottle of calming ylang-ylang essence had I dared hip Mrs. Captain of Industry III to the actual origins of her 'macrobiotic' California roll.

Don't get me wrong, I have plenty of happy memories from the time spent in Shri Devi's mercurial employ. On slow weekdays in August, with our clients decamped to vacation homes in the Hamptons, Minka would badger me until I consented to a leg wax or deep-pore cleansing, yelling that I was insulting her if I tried to get her to accept a bulging tip envelope in return for her complimentary services. "Please, Ayun, I am not a whore. Just let me shape your brows a bit with the hot wax. Just a tiny bit. This will be like gratuity for me, because I will be so happy that you look so much better."

Also, as a no-longer-self-employed massage therapist, I was spared the responsibility of hauling greasy sheets to the Laundromat. This meant a lot. Disorganized to the core, I'm hardly the type to stay abreast of my wash load, so back in the dining-room days, me finding out that I was out of clean sheets usually coincided with me finding out I was out of clean underwear. Off to the coin-op I'd toddle, totally skeeved out that my work-related laundry was commingling with my personal laundry. I was having horrible, visceral flashbacks to Showstopper Costumes, except there was no Gladys to take over midway through the gnarly task.

Oddly, the gruesome realities of the endlessly flawed human body never bother me when I've got someone on the massage table. Quite the opposite. My clients would probably be unnerved to hear it, but the very things they're embarrassed about are, more often than not, the things that cause me to regard them with tenderness, to consider them innocent little babes entirely worthy of compassionate touch (provided they tip well, of course). It's rare that I cotton to a gym-toned, clear-skinned, pleasantly scented twenty-two-year-old. Oh, I'll give her a good massage, but I probably won't admit her into my heart the way I will a furiously blushing, middle-aged farter with an inner tube of blub around his middle. Him, I practically feel compelled to rock in my arms, singing along to the Ladysmith Black Mambazo CD I prefer to bamboo flutes. I want to reassure him that it's okay. I'm a massage therapist. I've seen it all. Farting is as natural as sunrise, sunset, and the mid-massage erections that rise up to noticeably tent-pole the sheets, their horrified owners powerless to stop them. Jiggling flab, flaky lizard skin, nervous perspiration, weak chins, scars, wrinkles, birth defects, coffee breath, hirsutism, hair implants gone awry, a tendency to drool upon dozing off—I say bring it on! Kneading a cellulite-mottled haunch or spreading however many fingers happen to be on a gnarled hand (I've worked on as few as two, as many as six), my thoughts range from "What a piece of work is man" to "Fuck you, mainstream media!" It's very therapeutic for everyone involved. Hell, we're all imperfectly baked cakes, one eye canted lower than the other, noses sloshing astray of the midline. Sit at the head of a massage table and tell me if you don't agree. Even unclipped toenails, grody as they are, remind me of mankind's strangely reassuring inability to keep it all together. Okay, I prefer it when people's feet are clean, but I'm not going to throw stones about it, not when my apartment's made out of glass. Only later might it give me the heebie-jeebies, when whatever remains on the sheets—be it a stray short-'n'-curly, a funky aroma, or a mysterious stain—is residing in the tangled mountain of laundry containing my favorite jeans.

Don't tell me to get separate hampers. You get separate hampers if you're so smart! Or better yet, get a receptionist and tell her she's the one who has to wash those nasty sheets. That's what Shri Devi did, and it worked out great for me, if not for the poor girl hired to answer the phones, schedule appointments, and buck for tips on my behalf. At least she never had to scoop doodie up off the bathroom floor. Wait, neither did I. Just the other day, I was telling my husband about Felix Tatum's lavatory surprise, and he said, "Oh my god, what did you do with it?" You know, I can't remember. I probably just left it for somebody else to deal with. I like to think that picking up another's shit is where I draw the line, although I know there are people who do—usually unskilled laborers who haven't had the luxury of going to theater school before embarking on a life of professional drudgery. Whatever they're making, it isn't enough.

acknowledgments and apologia

What to Name Your Baby by Maxwell Nurnberg and Morris Rosenblum has proved invaluable in the fight to fudge up the identities of former coworkers and bosses currently working hard to remember me as well and as clearly as I remember them.

Here are the real names of some people who were a pleasure to work with and/or for: Agnes, Andy, Brooke, Carolyn, Dave, Drew, Ed, Ethel, Gayle-Ann, George, Jan, John, Jorge, Henry, Lois, Margaret, Mark, Mike O., Richard, Seana, Shawna, Stephen, Todd, Tom, and Tommy. I'd also like to reassure Susan that she is one of my all-time favorite massage clients and was never, not for a single second, a Lady Who Lunched.

Ain't nobody wield a hatchet like editor Leslie Miller—and if they do, I don't want to hear about it. Thanks to Krista Rafanello, Donna Stonecipher, and Dave Awl for their ongoing efforts in the dark arts of publicity, copyediting, and web design.

The readers of the *East Village Inky* have secret powers, and they're not afraid to use them, morphing time and again into a Special Guerrilla Marketeering Force on my behalf. I'm in their debt. Same goes for the independent booksellers who've gone out of their way to make me and my books feel welcome.

Thanks to Betsy Harris and Reed Halliday for never questioning their daughter's foolish decision to major in theater, and to the Neo-Futurists for keeping me in the game.

Finally, thank you to my husband, Greg Kotis, who wrote a play that banished day jobs for the time being and to our children, India (Teacher/Writer/Artist) and Milo (The Man Who Drives the Bus).

about the author

Ayun Halliday is the sole staff member of the quarterly zine *The East Village Inky* and the author of *The Big Rumpus: A Mother's Tale from the Trenches* and *No Touch Monkey! And Other Travel Lessons Learned Too Late.* She is *Bust* magazine's Mother Superior columnist and also contributes to NPR, *Hip Mama, Bitch,* and more anthologies than you can shake a stick at without dangling a participle. She can't facilitate a sexual release for you, but perhaps the next time you're in Brooklyn, she can give you a massage.

Dare to be Heinie. Visit www.ayunhalliday.com.

selected titles from seal press